This Journal
Belongs to

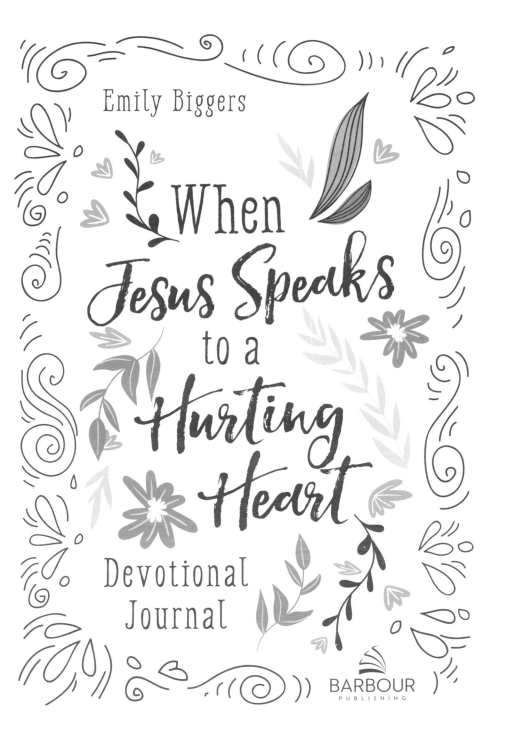

Emily Biggers

When Jesus Speaks to a Hurting Heart

Devotional Journal

BARBOUR
PUBLISHING

Published by Barbour Publishing, Inc., 1810 Barbour Drive, Uhrichsville, Ohio 44683, www.barbourbooks.com

Our mission is to inspire the world with the life-changing message of the Bible.

Member of the
Evangelical Christian
Publishers Association

Printed in China.

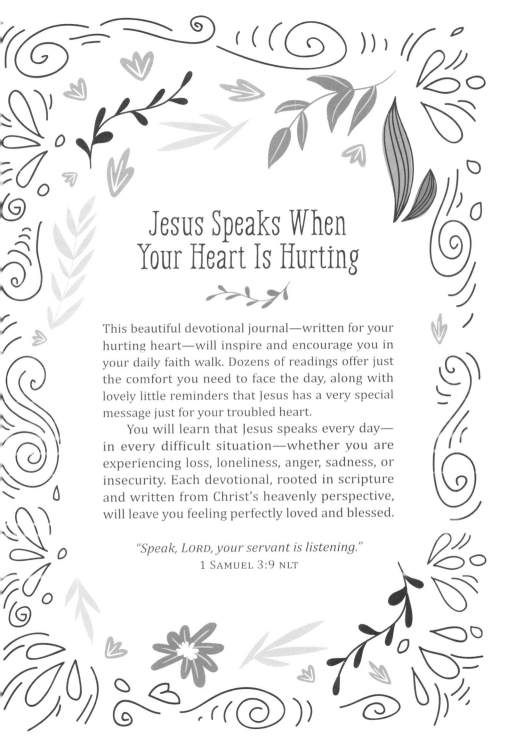

Jesus Speaks When
Your Heart Is Hurting

This beautiful devotional journal—written for your
hurting heart—will inspire and encourage you in
your daily faith walk. Dozens of readings offer just
the comfort you need to face the day, along with
lovely little reminders that Jesus has a very special
message just for your troubled heart.

You will learn that Jesus speaks every day—
in every difficult situation—whether you are
experiencing loss, loneliness, anger, sadness, or
insecurity. Each devotional, rooted in scripture
and written from Christ's heavenly perspective,
will leave you feeling perfectly loved and blessed.

"Speak, LORD, your servant is listening."
1 SAMUEL 3:9 NLT

Worth the Wait

You have never cried a tear that I did not see. You are My precious one. I loved you enough to die for you. Do you trust that I have not forgotten you? I never will.

I have given mankind free will, and people make choices. Some of these choices wound you deeply. This is part of living in a fallen world.

The good news is that I am with you. I am right there, even on the saddest day of your life. I am with the brokenhearted. I am closest when you are saddest. I will bind up your wounds. I will listen. I will hold you close.

I save every tear that you cry, and one day, in heaven, there will be no more tears. You will never cry again. It is a glorious place that is worth the wait.

....

....

....

....

....

....

....

....

....

....

You keep track of all my sorrows. You have collected all my tears in your bottle. You have recorded each one in your book.
Psalm 56:8 nlt

Pure Light

You know about dark valleys. You sense the shadow of death. Yet you still see that glimmer of light, don't you? Each day brings just enough hope to carry you through to the next. This is because I am with you. I am behind every bright spot in your path. I orchestrate those little blessings that seem too good to be true. There is no coincidence for the person of faith.

I am the Good Shepherd and you are My sheep. I look after you with tender care. I never let you out of My line of vision. Learn the sound of My voice so that I may direct you all the days of your life.

As you face darkness, remember that I am pure light. I will be your boldness when you need bravery and your comfort when you feel you can't go on. You never walk alone.

Even if I walk through a very dark valley, I will not be afraid, because you are with me. Your rod and your shepherd's staff comfort me.
PSALM 23:4 NCV

Look Up

Anxiety is a trick the enemy uses to make you think you need to worry. He is always prowling about, scheming and attempting to distract believers from the truth. The truth is that I am always with you, so there is no reason to fear.

Do not look toward tomorrow with a furrowed brow and eyes full of worry. I am holding your hand and I will pour into you exactly the measure of strength you need to pass through each trial. Trust Me. We will take it one day at a time, one step at a time.

When you feel overwhelmed, remember that you are not alone. I will not just give you strength. I will *be* your strength. There is no need to fear, child. Look up. I am right here at your side, and I will never desert you.

....

....

....

....

....

....

....

....

"So do not fear, for I am with you; do not be dismayed,
for I am your God. I will strengthen you and help you;
I will uphold you with my righteous right hand."
Isaiah 41:10 niv

In My Hands

I saw you before you were formed in your mother's womb. You were, and are, a delightful thought to Me. Every day ordained for you is a gift. I could not love you more if I tried.

Nothing touches your life that has not been filtered through My fingers. I care deeply for you and it hurts Me to see you hurt. Certainly, there are trials in your life. I have allowed them. You don't understand the struggles. It is nearly impossible for you to welcome them. But as they come, rest in Me. Know that I always have your best interest at heart. Know that the trial is temporary. It will pass with time.

I am your Savior, your Redeemer, your Friend. Your life is in My hands—and these are the hands of One who loves you with an unfailing love. Life will hurt at times. Trust that I am still in control and I will never give you more than you can bear.

....

....

....

....

....

....

....

....

Lord, I trust you. I have said,
"You are my God." My life is in your hands.
Psalm 31:14–15 ncv

Even in Silence

There are times when I will not speak. These are days to draw nearer to Me and simply trust. Read My Word. The pages of scripture will lift your spirits and focus your eyes upon Me once more. Look around at the blessings in your life. I will reveal Myself to you even in My silence.

There are times when I will not move. This does not mean you will be stuck forever in the circumstances that are bringing you discomfort. Have faith. The storm will end, or I will carry you through it.

I may take you through a trial so that you can grow and learn. But I will always bring you out. I am your Provider and your Savior. Nothing can snatch you out of My hand. In this world you will certainly have trouble. But I have overcome the world, child, and you belong to Me. I will always rescue you at just the right time.

....

....

....

....

....

....

....

....

....

....

He brought me out into a spacious place;
he rescued me because he delighted in me.
PSALM 18:19 NIV

Always Faithful

I will always be faithful. It is not in My character to be anything less.

If it seems I am not there, you have moved away from Me. Turn around. Take a step. Look up. I am here. I am the one thing in your life that is constant. I never change. I am the same yesterday, today, and tomorrow.

As you move through days that are a struggle, hold on. Hold steady. Hold tight. Gaze upon Me, for I am truth and light. I am the only way through the chaos. Don't get caught up in worrying about tomorrow or the next day. Just take the next step and do the next right thing. I am working things out for you.

I long for you to trust in My promises. When you hope in Me, you can experience true rest. Never doubt My faithfulness.

....

....

....

....

....

....

....

....

....

....

Let us hold unswervingly to the hope we profess,
for he who promised is faithful.
HEBREWS 10:23 NIV

Rescued

Sometimes I calm the storm. Sometimes I call you out to walk upon the waves. Trust in Me and I will always come through for you. It may not be instant, for My timing is rarely what you may want it to be. But I will always, *always* come through.

There will be days when you think the waters are too deep and that you will surely drown. It is on those days that you simply cannot trust your feelings. You must lean in hard to your faith. You must remember that I see you. I never lose sight of where you are. I do not like to watch you struggle, but sometimes I allow it for a season.

On your darkest day, in your deepest crisis, when you cannot take one more step, I am near. I will take hold of you. I will rescue you. I will see you through to the other side. Trust Me.

....

....

....

....

....

....

....

....

....

....

He reached down from on high and took hold of me;
he drew me out of deep waters.
Psalm 18:16 niv

Burden-Bearer

You are not meant to bear your own burdens, child. That is a lie the prince of darkness tries to sell you. Reject it! I hear your cries late at night. I see the worry that consumes you. I desire for you to cast your cares upon Me, and yet you insist on holding on to them.

I am stronger than you are. Your burdens are not overwhelming to Me. Give them to Me. Let Me carry them for you. I long to see you stand up straight again, unencumbered by this giant load. I want you to be free of these cares that cloud your vision of the future. I want your step to be light and your eyes to be bright once again.

I will carry your troubles for you. I will sort them out, if you will let Me. I love you and I want to be your Burden-Bearer today and every day.

Give your burdens to the LORD, and he will take care of you.
He will not permit the godly to slip and fall.
PSALM 55:22 NLT

My Best for You

I have heard you call out, questioning why. I have seen your thoughts—the ones that question whether I am real, whether I care, and if so, why I am allowing you to hurt.

You are not seeing the full picture right now. You only see what you want—I see what you need. Remember that dream you were chasing that could have led you to destruction? I put a barrier in your path in just the nick of time. You were angry and hurt. Understand that I put that obstacle there for your own good.

Know that I have great plans for you. Some of the plans may require that you hurt a little in the present to receive what I have for you in the future. It will be worth it.

Trust that I am working all things together for your good. My immense love for you could never wish you harm. I am not a withholder of any good gift. All of My ways are right. You have a very bright future, My child.

....

....

....

....

....

....

....

....

"For I know the plans I have for you," says the LORD. "They are plans for good and not for disaster, to give you a future and a hope."
JEREMIAH 29:11 NLT

Assurance and Peace

I know you are afraid. You cannot hide your fear from Me. I know you through and through, for I knit you together in your mother's womb. I have called you My own, and that will never change. Nothing is able to snatch you from Me. I long for you to take every worrisome thought captive and bring it to Me. Allow Me to replace fear with assurance and anxiety with peace.

I see your worry, but you must take the step toward Me. You must make the choice to cast your cares upon Me. Like My disciples during a raging storm on the boat, your faith wavers. It is sure one moment, but lacking the next. Ask Me to increase your faith, and I will. I stand ready to help, ready to rescue, and ready to comfort.

Release all your troubles to Me. Trust Me, dear one. I am here for you, and I will never let you down.

....

....

....

....

....

....

....

....

....

"Don't let your hearts be troubled. Trust in God, and trust also in me."
JOHN 14:1 NLT

Remember This

All around you are people who put their trust in the world. They will always come up empty-handed. They will always be lacking and insecure. The world is not your home, child, and there is nothing there for you to trust in. Remember this.

You may not see golden statues on every corner, although there are some who worship such idols. Many of the gods in your society are subtle. They are entertainment and wealth and beauty. They are status and travel and technology. They can be good things taken too far, or creations that are taking the place of the Creator. Children, work, or success can become an idol.

Put your trust in Me alone. I am the God of Abraham and Isaac and Jacob. I am the same yesterday, today, and tomorrow. I am the Father, the Son, and the Holy Spirit. I have come that you may have life—abundant, eternal, and free.

....
....
....
....
....
....
....
....

"Do not worship idols or make statues or gods
for yourselves. I am the LORD your God."
LEVITICUS 19:4 NCV

Rest in Me

Each day you have a chance to start over, an opportunity to focus on Me and give Me control. I know your heart is hurting. I know some days it is all you can do to get out of bed. You seek to control the few things left in your life that you think you can.

It is so tiring to live that way. I don't want you to be exhausted, spinning your wheels day and night, working hard to exist on your own. I want you to rest. I want you to relinquish control and put your faith in Me. Try trusting Me with just the next moment. In time, as you see Me come through for you, you will be able to trust Me with an hour, then a day.

I am trustworthy. You will see.

....
....
....
....
....
....
....
....
....
....

Trust the LORD with all your heart, and don't
depend on your own understanding. Remember the
LORD in all you do, and he will give you success.
PROVERBS 3:5–6 NCV

Embrace the Storm

As a human being, you are limited in your understanding. What may appear to be the worst thing imaginable may end up being the best thing for you.

I have used rain to bless and to curse, haven't I? Storms in your life are the same. They are allowed by My hand. No storm can touch you except the ones I permit.

I know that the middle of a storm is a scary place to be, but if you know you are in My hand, you have nothing to fear. Embrace the storm to the best of your ability. Ask Me to carry you through it. Don't resist it. It may be that the road straight through the center of your current storm is the pathway to peace.

It is the trials in your life that shape and mature you, develop your character, and cause your faith to deepen.

*"He uses the clouds to punish people
or to water his earth and show his love."*
JOB 37:13 NCV

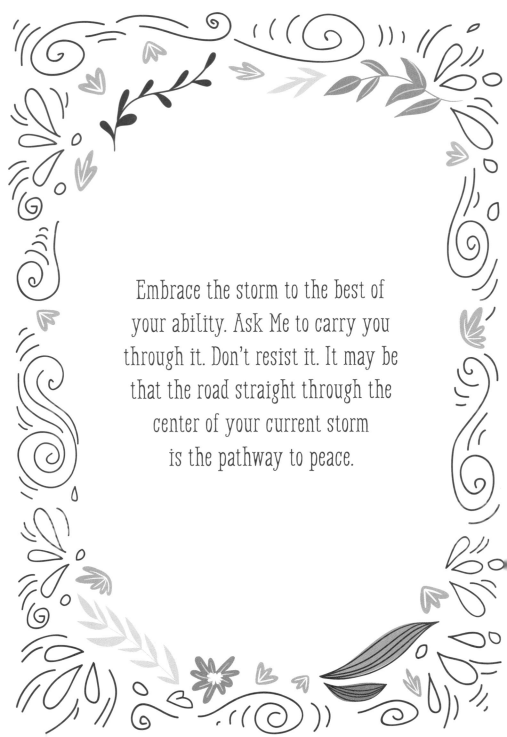

Embrace the storm to the best of
your ability. Ask Me to carry you
through it. Don't resist it. It may be
that the road straight through the
center of your current storm
is the pathway to peace.

Rise Up

When you wake up when it is still dark outside, I am here. When you toss and turn, turn to Me. There is no hour too early or too late. I do not sleep, nor do I slumber. I am always watching over you, always here.

Sometimes I wake you up. I call to you to read My Word, to seek Me in prayer, to find Me in the wee hours of the night when all is still and quiet. If you sense that I am calling you, rise up like young Samuel did. He thought it was Eli who called to him, but it was Me, his God.

You may not hear My voice audibly, but you will sense it in your spirit. Heed the calling. I may have something to encourage your heart that you will miss if you don't answer right away, even if it costs you some sleep.

I rise before dawn and cry for help; I have put my hope in your word. My eyes stay open through the watches of the night, that I may meditate on your promises.
Psalm 119:147–148 niv

Run to Me

One day grief will be a thing of the past. You will hardly remember it and you will never again experience its weight. In heaven, death and pain will cease to exist. There will be no more tears.

But I speak here of the future when you are with Me in glory. This is not your human experience. The losses you have been dealt are no small matter. They have cut you to your core and left you questioning My love for you. Rest assured that I have not removed My hand from your life. I love you with all of My heart and I always will.

Run toward Me in your grief—don't turn away from Me. In your mourning, you are weak, but in your weakness, I am strong. I want to be your Strength and your Comfort.

....

....

....

....

....

....

....

....

....

" 'He will wipe every tear from their eyes. There will
be no more death' or mourning or crying or pain,
for the old order of things has passed away."
REVELATION 21:4 NIV

In Your Brokenness

When you were hidden in your mother's womb, your tiny heart beat strong and alive. I protected that heart and prepared it for the cold, frightening world it would soon face. You entered a fallen world the day you were born. In it are things that will break your heart. I would love to keep you from this, but for reasons you cannot understand right now, I allow it.

It wounds Me when one of My children has a broken heart. I take no pleasure in seeing those whom the Father has entrusted to Me hurt. I am touched by your gut-wrenching cries and your somber countenance where I once delighted in your smile. I hurt when you hurt.

I will draw close to you in your brokenness. I am the care flight that comes to the rescue when your spirit is crushed. You may bear a broken heart more than once in this life, but you will never bear it alone.

....

....

....

....

....

....

....

....

....

The LORD is close to the brokenhearted, and he
saves those whose spirits have been crushed.
PSALM 34:18 NCV

Carry You

Let's make a trade, you and I. How does this sound? You give Me your burdens, and in return, I will give you rest.

Sometimes you convince yourself that you have something to prove. You think you must do it all on your own. But no one has called you to be a superhero. No one expects the supernatural from you. There is only so much that one soul can bear.

Isn't it time to rest? Doesn't that sound appealing, child? Let Me take it from here. Lay down your load. I've got you covered. In fact, I will carry not just your burdens; I will carry *you* as well. It is time you found some rest for your soul. Allow Me to be your rest.

....
....
....
....
....
....
....
....
....

"Come to me, all of you who are tired and have heavy loads, and I will give you rest. Accept my teachings and learn from me, because I am gentle and humble in spirit, and you will find rest for your lives."
MATTHEW 11:28–29 NCV

Seasons

You may cry in the night, but joy comes in the morning. There is always relief for sorrow. Even after the darkest night, there is always a new dawn. Though the thunder may be so strong it shakes you to your very soul, every storm will pass.

I love you too much to leave you in sorrow. I will come to you. In due time, this current trial will be a distant memory. While you may bear some scars from the battle, you will no longer be on the front lines fighting for your next breath.

There is a time for everything, and you will not remain in one season forever. Just as I allow the harshness of winter, there is also the promise of spring.

Have faith. This period of hardship will give way to joy again in time.

....

....

....

....

....

....

....

....

For no one is cast off by the Lord forever. Though he brings grief,
he will show compassion, so great is his unfailing love. For he
does not willingly bring affliction or grief to anyone.
LAMENTATIONS 3:31–33 NIV

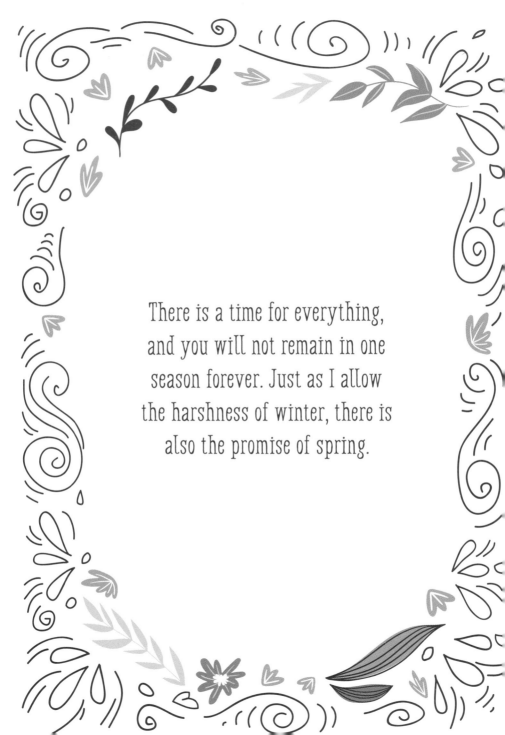

There is a time for everything,
and you will not remain in one
season forever. Just as I allow
the harshness of winter, there is
also the promise of spring.

No Limits

When you feel like you have lost the battle, remember that I have labeled you "more than a conqueror."

Nothing you can do and nothing that can be done to you is stronger than My love. I am more powerful than any pull on your heartstrings, any tug at your allegiance. Demons flee at the mention of My name. They have no choice. My grace spills out and floods over you. There is no limit to My favor and forgiveness for those whom I have called My own.

When you feel alone, reject that deceiving feeling. Nothing can separate you from My love.

....

....

....

....

....

....

....

....

....

....

No, in all these things we are more than conquerors through him who loved us. For I am convinced that neither death nor life, neither angels nor demons, neither the present nor the future, nor any powers, neither height nor depth, nor anything else in all creation, will be able to separate us from the love of God that is in Christ Jesus our Lord.
ROMANS 8:37–39 NIV

Be There

You must forgive as you have been forgiven and love as you have been loved. Perhaps most importantly, you must comfort others, child, in the way you have received comfort.

Remember My hand upon your tired brow. When you come across another weary soul, be there. You don't have to have the right words. You just have to show up as I have shown up for you.

I take delight in comforting you. I love to see the corners of your mouth turn up ever so slightly to form the beginning of a smile.

When you have found your way again, look to the left and the right on the narrow path you walk. When you see someone struggling as you have struggled, be there.

....

....

....

....

....

....

....

....

All praise to God, the Father of our Lord Jesus Christ. God is our merciful Father and the source of all comfort. He comforts us in all our troubles so that we can comfort others. When they are troubled, we will be able to give them the same comfort God has given us.
2 CORINTHIANS 1:3–4 NLT

True to My Word

I want to be enough for you. I long for you to rest in Me and trust Me just for this day, this hour, this moment. It may seem like I have left you all alone, but I haven't. I have promised never to leave or forsake you, and I am always true to My Word.

The world screams for you to throw caution to the wind and do whatever makes you happy. It tells you that things should happen instantly, that success comes overnight. These are not My ways. Oftentimes, I work behind the scenes. My timetable is not the same as yours. Trust Me. I have not forgotten you.

My grace is sufficient for you today. Rely on Me.

....

....

....

....

....

....

....

....

....

....

And He said to me, "My grace is sufficient for you, for My strength is made perfect in weakness." Therefore most gladly I will rather boast in my infirmities, that the power of Christ may rest upon me.
2 CORINTHIANS 12:9 NKJV

Keep Believing

Stay the course, My child. Do not veer to the left or the right. Stay strong in your faith. Believe that I am good and that I only want the very best for you. I have given you abundant and eternal life through your faith. I am the Way, the Truth, and the Life. No one comes to God except through Me.

You are not of this world, but you are in it. You are an alien in a land that has many traps and snares from the evil one. While you must exist in the world, you draw your daily sustenance from Me. You belong to Me. Keep on believing. Keep on seeking Me. I am always here—I will never leave you.

....

....

....

....

....

....

....

....

....

....

....

....

But you must continue to believe this truth and stand firmly in it. Don't drift away from the assurance you received when you heard the Good News. The Good News has been preached all over the world, and I, Paul, have been appointed as God's servant to proclaim it.
Colossians 1:23 nlt

Hope Is Eternal

You will have trouble in this world. I have not promised you a trouble-free life. But I do assure you of My presence all along the way.

You are developing perseverance because of your present trial. Your character is being strengthened. You will suffer for a little while, but you have eternal hope in Me. You will never be without hope. As a believer, you are not hopeless, but hopeful. Trust in Me to get you through this trial and bring you out on the other side. You have the gift of the Holy Spirit, the Comforter and Counselor. Find hope in the Spirit of God. That is a hope that will never let you down.

....

....

....

....

....

....

....

....

We also have joy with our troubles, because we know that these troubles produce patience. And patience produces character, and character produces hope. And this hope will never disappoint us, because God has poured out his love to fill our hearts. He gave us his love through the Holy Spirit, whom God has given to us.
ROMANS 5:3–5 NCV

My Name

When you cannot pray, just speak My name. There is power in the name of your Savior. Speak My name, *Jesus*, and I will come close. I will comfort you. I will fight your battles for you, and I will give you rest.

I am always faithful, loving, and true. Some people look for success and contentment in the world. They seek the next thrill, the next adventure. Some go from relationship to relationship, looking for love. Others try to find their worth in money and possessions. You have been spared this. You have found true peace, true hope. You have found it through your walk with Me.

When you have no other words, speak My name. My grace is sufficient for you. In every circumstance, I am always enough.

....

....

....

....

....

....

....

....

....

Therefore God exalted him to the highest place and gave him the name
that is above every name, that at the name of Jesus every knee should
bow, in heaven and on earth and under the earth, and every tongue
acknowledge that Jesus Christ is Lord, to the glory of God the Father.
PHILIPPIANS 2:9–11 NIV

Great Delight

I take great delight in your praise, child. I love to hear you sing to Me and praise My name. The sweetest songs are the ones you sing when your heart is hurting. You choose to praise Me in the midst of the storm rather than waiting until the sun comes out again. While the tempest rages on, you call out to Me. You remember that you belong to Me. You give Me glory even while you are in pain.

Never be afraid to trust and praise Me, even when you don't feel like it. Feelings come and go, but I am constant. I am the same yesterday and today. Tomorrow and the next day and the day after that, I will still love you more than you can imagine. Choose to praise Me on good days and bad alike. I love you, child.

Why, my soul, are you downcast? Why so disturbed within me?
Put your hope in God, for I will yet praise him, my Savior and my God.
PSALM 42:5 NIV

Never be afraid to trust and praise Me, even when you don't feel like it. Feelings come and go, but I am constant. I am the same yesterday and today.

In Any Circumstance

Are you lacking? Child, this is the human condition. There will always be a longing unfulfilled. As soon as one blessing comes into your life, you begin noticing another area that is not as you want it to be.

The secret is learning to praise your God in any circumstance. The apostle Paul learned this. He was content in any situation—whether he had plenty or was in need.

I know that life is not as you imagined it would be. I want to fill in the gaps with My peace, so much so that you look up and realize that while your circumstances may not have changed, your heart has. Let Me train your heart to be content.

....

....

....

....

....

....

....

....

....

Though the fig tree may not blossom, nor fruit be on the vines; though the labor of the olive may fail, and the fields yield no food; though the flock may be cut off from the fold, and there be no herd in the stalls— yet I will rejoice in the LORD, I will joy in the God of my salvation.
HABAKKUK 3:17–18 NKJV

What You Need

Waiting is hard, isn't it? It is difficult to hope for that which you cannot see. In your season of waiting, know that I am growing you and preparing you. I am strengthening you.

It is tempting to compare your life to that of another. Resist this temptation, child. You have not walked in another's shoes. You don't know his or her inner struggles. No one has a perfect life. There are holes in every heart that can only truly be filled by My presence.

Sometimes the answer to your prayers is yes, and sometimes I say no. Other times I will call you to wait. I often have a special gift in store for you at the end of your waiting. Cling to My promises and trust in Me. I withhold no good and perfect gift. I give you what you need when you need it.

Wait on the Lord; be of good courage, and He shall strengthen your heart; wait, I say, on the Lord!
Psalm 27:14 nkjv

My Beloved

You are not a slave to fear. You have been sealed with the Holy Spirit, making you a child of God. When fear begins to creep into your mind, recognize it for what it is. Fear is Satan's attempt to make you believe that your God is small, rather than the King of Glory. Fear starts small, and if you allow it to take root, it will grow like ivy, taking over your heart. Cut it off when you first recognize it. Speak My name over it. Call it what it is: a lie from the pit of hell.

Remember that you belong to Me. You have been adopted into God's family. Write it down. Speak it aloud. Claim your identity in the Lord of lords. You are made righteous through My death on the cross. You are My beloved, and you have absolutely nothing to fear.

....

....

....

....

....

....

....

....

....

For you did not receive the spirit of bondage again to fear, but you received the Spirit of adoption by whom we cry out, "Abba, Father."
ROMANS 8:15 NKJV

In the Moment

When you look back, you are filled with regret. When you look ahead, fear overwhelms you. When you spend too much time focusing on the past or the future, you miss the blessings I want to give you in this moment.

I am the Redeemer of your past. Nothing you have done is too big for Me to forgive. I have cast your sin as far as the east is from the west. It is not worth going over and over again in your mind. I am not dwelling on your past. I am looking at a redeemed child of the living God. I am excited about where we are going together.

The future is bright for you. I promised you that I have good plans for your life. Trust in this. Trust in Me. I am the Redeemer of lost time.

....

....

....

....

....

....

....

....

....

....

"So I will restore to you the years that the swarming locust has eaten, the crawling locust, the consuming locust, and the chewing locust, My great army which I sent among you."
JOEL 2:25 NKJV

Treasured and Loved

I love the spots of the cheetah and the stripes of the zebra. The trees are gloriously green in spring, and I love to clothe them in reds and yellows in autumn. But no other creation compares to man. Mankind is My masterpiece, created in My image.

You, My child, bring Me great joy. I love to watch you go about your days. I marvel at the way you use the abilities I have given you. You are a delight to Me.

On your darkest day, in your hardest hour, remember that I created you, I breathed My life into you. You are treasured and loved. You are never alone and never forsaken. I love you beyond any concept of love that you have. I don't expect you to be perfect, and I am here to help you start again when you mess up. Take My hand and know that I am always here for you.

....

....

....

....

....

....

....

....

....

For we are God's masterpiece. He has created us anew in Christ Jesus,
so we can do the good things he planned for us long ago.
EPHESIANS 2:10 NLT

I don't expect you to be perfect,
and I am here to help you
start again when you mess up.
Take My hand and know that
I am always here for you.

Power

There is power in My Word. You may read and study it all your life, yet never fully understand its power. The power is found in meditating upon My Word. Turn it over in your mind. Wrestle with it. Chew on it; let it digest, slowly becoming not just words, but part of you. Meditate on My truths, child. Cling to My promises. Internalize scripture as if your life depends on it. . .because it does.

There will be a day when believers are persecuted in a greater way than has ever been experienced. Write My Word on your heart so that you are prepared when others come against you. Know My Word so you will recognize false teachers and doctrines when they are presented to you.

There is power in My Word that can turn your day around in a heartbeat. Don't leave that power source untapped today.

"Keep this Book of the Law always on your lips; meditate on it day and night, so that you may be careful to do everything written in it. Then you will be prosperous and successful."
Joshua 1:8 niv

Your Healer

She reached out to touch the hem of My robe. What faith that woman had. She had suffered a bleeding disease for twelve long years, and she was desperate. She heard I was the Son of God. She knew I had healed others. She believed.

I instantly knew she had touched Me. She was instantly healed. It was her faith that made her well.

What burden do you bear? What is it that you carry? Have you lost something that brought you great joy? Has anger overtaken your mind and heart? Do you believe that I am powerful enough to heal your hurting heart? I am.

Come close, My child. Touch the hem of My robe. I am waiting to be your Healer.

....

....

....

....

....

....

....

....

*When she heard about Jesus, she came up behind him in the crowd
and touched his cloak, because she thought, "If I just touch his
clothes, I will be healed." Immediately her bleeding stopped and she
felt in her body that she was freed from her suffering.*
MARK 5:27–29 NIV

Always Right

My thoughts and ways are higher than yours. Do not try to understand—you can't right now.

Mary questioned Me. She knew I loved Lazarus and could have kept him from dying, and yet. . .I didn't. She wondered why I hadn't come sooner.

I know you might feel like I have left you when I allow tragedy or loss in your life.

Believe Me that when you feel forgotten, nothing is further from the truth.

I may not always do what you desire, but My ways are always right. Find hope in the fact that I am always on time—never early or late. I act and refrain from acting. I heal and I allow sickness. I provide another breath. . .until I take each of My children home to heaven.

Where am I when bad things happen? I am right there with you, child.

....

....

....

....

....

....

....

....

When Mary arrived and saw Jesus, she fell at his feet and said,
"Lord, if only you had been here, my brother would not have died."
JOHN 11:32 NLT

In the Bright Spots

The lepers were ostracized, avoided, and feared. Yet I still touched them. Their lesions were healed and they were free to live among others again. They were given a new life. Only one came back to thank Me that day. Just one out of the ten men who were healed.

Do you thank Me, child? Do you turn to Me when I answer your prayers?

I will meet your needs. Nothing is too big or small for Me to take care of. Look for Me in the little things—that friend who reached out at just the right moment. Your coworker who picked up some of the slack on the very day you needed it most. I am in the moments of relief. I am in the blessings and the bright spots.

See Me there. Thank Me, child. Be like the one leper who turned back, the one who recognized the source of his healing.

....

....

....

....

....

....

....

....

....

One of them, when he saw that he was healed,
came back to Jesus, shouting, "Praise God!"
LUKE 17:15 NLT

Healing

What deficiency do you bear? What insecurity has plagued you for so long you can't even trace its origin?

The blind man at the pool of Siloam could not see. He was born that way, but I healed him. He came to Me and I gave him instructions, which he followed. He followed My directions in faith. He trusted Me.

Call on Me. Seek Me. I am still in the business of healing. I long to take away all that plagues you, all that limits you and holds you back. I long to heal you of the hurts and habits and hang-ups that have become strongholds in your life.

I may not put mud upon your eyes or send you to a river. Perhaps your wound is one of the heart rather than a physical disability. I am also a heart healer, child. Give Me your burden and trust Me. Healing is nearer than you may imagine possible.

....
....
....
....
....
....
....

He told them, "The man they call Jesus made mud and spread it over my eyes and told me, 'Go to the pool of Siloam and wash yourself.' So I went and washed, and now I can see!"
JOHN 9:11 NLT

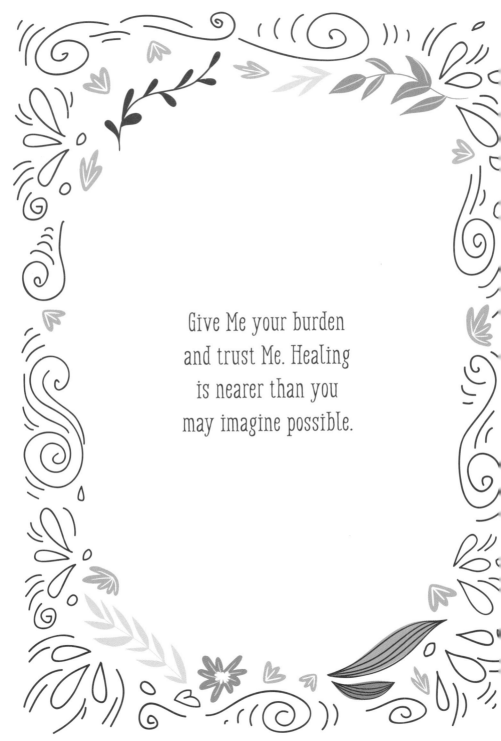

Give Me your burden
and trust Me. Healing
is nearer than you
may imagine possible.

Sufficient

Just as I called the tax collector down from the sycamore tree, I call to you now, child. I want to fellowship with you.

I am not concerned about your sin. I died for you while you were yet a sinner. I covered all of your sin—past, present, and future. My blood was enough.

You don't need to hide anything from Me. I can help you with the areas of your life you are not proud of, the addictions you cannot shake, and the sin that entangles you.

If you don't feel good enough, remember Zacchaeus. He was a criminal, a thief among men, but I met him where he was. I called him down from the tree and walked home with him that day.

You don't have to be enough. I am your enough. My grace is sufficient.

....

....

....

....

....

....

....

....

Meanwhile, Zacchaeus stood before the Lord and said, "I will give half my wealth to the poor, Lord, and if I have cheated people on their taxes, I will give them back four times as much!"
LUKE 19:8 NLT

Accept the Answer

I know all about earnest prayer. I prayed to My Father from Gethsemane. I cried out to Him, asking that the cup be taken from Me. Was there another way? Was there a way out? Could another plan be put into place? If so, I wanted Him to save Me in those moments.

I prayed hard that night in the garden. I longed for God to alter the plan of salvation, but it wasn't meant to be. He answered My prayer. The cup was Mine. The answer was that I was the Lamb, the provision for mankind to be made right with God. I was willing—I did not have to be dragged. I went to Calvary of My own accord. I answered the call and fulfilled the prophecy. I died for all humanity.

When it seems as if I do not answer your prayers, know that I do. Pray for My will, and accept the answer. You will not always understand, but you can choose to accept.

....
....
....
....
....
....
....
....
....

And being in anguish, he prayed more earnestly,
and his sweat was like drops of blood falling to the ground.
LUKE 22:44 NIV

When you come to Me with requests,
sometimes it may seem like I do
not answer, but I always hear your
prayers, and I always answer.

Much More. . .

The man couldn't walk. He was lowered down on a mat through the roof and laid before Me. His friends loved this afflicted man enough to find a way to get him to Me through the crowd! It was amazing. The request was that I make this lame man walk.

I did much more than that—I also forgave his sins. The Pharisees and teachers of the law were appalled that I would do so, thus claiming to be the Son of God. But I could not merely heal his body and allow his spirit to remain dark and separated from My Father!

When you come to Me with requests, sometimes it may seem like I do not answer, but I always hear your prayers, and I always answer. Sometimes I may be at work on your spirit, which is far more important to Me than your temporary physical needs. Trust Me. I long to bring healing to you, child, in every way you can imagine—and beyond.

....

....

....

....

....

....

....

....

....

When Jesus saw their faith, he said to the
paralyzed man, "Son, your sins are forgiven."
MARK 2:5 NIV

Speak Life

That old saying about sticks and stones isn't true, is it? Words hurt. You chanted as a child that "words will never hurt me," but you knew even then that it was not true. Unkind words penetrate to the core of your being, and some hang around in your memory for a long, long time.

When someone's words wound you, try to think about the speaker's heart. Is he hurting? Is she insecure? Many times when someone tears another person down, this is the case.

It may help a little just to consider the hurting heart behind the hurtful words. It is hard to turn the other cheek. It is sometimes nearly impossible to forgive. But it is My call on your life. It is My way—the way of forgiveness.

Today, choose to use your words to speak life and not death into others' lives. When you are spoken to harshly, pray for the one who wounds you with her words.

....
....
....
....
....
....
....
....

The words of the reckless pierce like swords,
but the tongue of the wise brings healing.
PROVERBS 12:18 NIV

None Too Great

Do you remember how I cast the demons from those who were possessed? I removed them from a man called Legion, and I cast them into a nearby herd of swine that then ran wildly into the water and were drowned.

Is there a stronghold in your life that you just can't break free from? There is no demon, no stronghold, no power too great for Me to conquer in your life. Lay down the control. Ask Me to remove whatever it is that hinders you. I want you to run the race freely. I want you to be unencumbered by besetting sin and Satan's lies.

Legion had his name because "they were many," but I proved that they were not too many for Me. I am your powerful Savior, and I stand ready to battle the demons in your life as well.

The man from whom the demons had gone out begged to go with him, but Jesus sent him away, saying, "Return home and tell how much God has done for you." So the man went away and told all over town how much Jesus had done for him.

Luke 8:38–39 niv

For the Good

People will let you down. Even those with the best intentions are only human. Learn to accept that the people you love possess flaws just as you do. Even your Christian friends and family members are in a constant battle between the spirit and the flesh. Sometimes one wins out and sometimes the other.

Refrain from keeping a record of wrongs. Love is quick to forgive. Remember that those who forgive others will in turn be forgiven by their heavenly Father. Because you have been a recipient of grace, be generous with mercy yourself.

I do not call you to allow abuse. Establish boundaries when you need to, in order to keep from being hurt repeatedly by the same individual. But remember that people will, at times, hurt you. It is inevitable. Choose to look for the good in everyone—even those who disappoint you.

Our sinful selves want what is against the Spirit, and the Spirit wants what is against our sinful selves. The two are against each other, so you cannot do just what you please.
Galatians 5:17 NCV

Provision

Are you concerned about your finances? I know it seems there is never enough money. Lay down your financial burdens at My throne. Work hard and avoid unnecessary debt. Leave the rest to Me. Remember how many times in the past money has shown up at just the right time?

If you sense that you are beginning to look to money or material things more than you look to Me, beware. The love of money can be a subtle trap. You cannot serve two masters. You are in the world, but as My child, you are not of it. You are just passing through. Heaven is your home.

Day by day I will provide what is needed. Ask Me for your daily bread. I am concerned with every area of your life—even your money. I am able to provide. Trust Me.

....

....

....

....

....

....

....

....

....

....

*Keep your lives free from the love of money and be
content with what you have, because God has said,
"Never will I leave you; never will I forsake you."*
HEBREWS 13:5 NIV

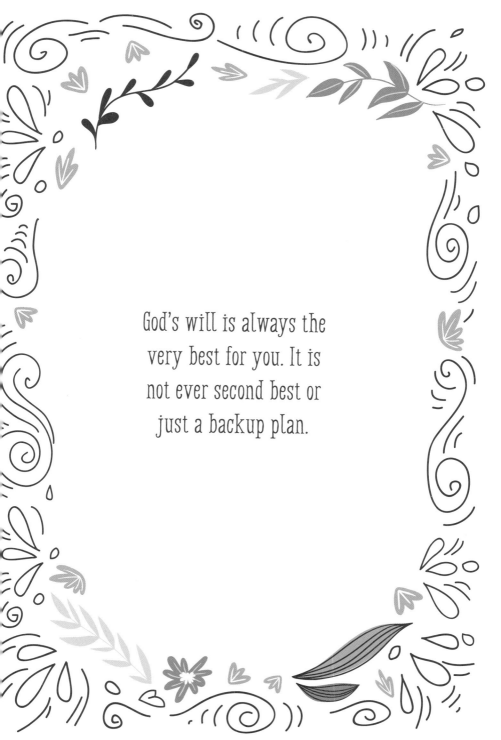

God's will is always the
very best for you. It is
not ever second best or
just a backup plan.

The Best for You

When you feel you cannot pray, I understand, child. This is a common reaction when people are hurting.

You know that I am one with the Father and with the Spirit. In a mysterious way, we are three and yet one and the same. The job of the Holy Spirit is to intercede for you. The Spirit takes your needs before the Father in accordance with His will.

God's will is always the very best for you. It is not ever second best or just a backup plan. The Holy Spirit knows your thoughts and takes your needs before God. Just speak My name. Just rest and allow the Spirit to work on your behalf.

....

....

....

....

....

....

....

....

....

In the same way, the Spirit helps us in our weakness. We do not know what we ought to pray for, but the Spirit himself intercedes for us through wordless groans. And he who searches our hearts knows the mind of the Spirit, because the Spirit intercedes for God's people in accordance with the will of God.
ROMANS 8:26–27 NIV

Heaven's Glory

The life you live on earth is temporary. When you pass through the veil to the other side, you will experience the glory of heaven. Then you will see fully what you can only understand in part right now.

In the midst of your present trial, remember that your pain is temporal, but your life is eternal. Your suffering will seem like nothing once you enter the magnificent mansion in heaven that I have gone to prepare for you.

Some days you wonder whether or not it is worth it—the Christian walk, the narrow road. It is worth it. In the blink of an eye one day glory will be revealed and you will never look back to your life on earth where things were imperfect and broken. When you are in paradise with Me, all things will be right. For now, trust in Me and allow Me to carry you through this trial.

....

....

....

....

....

....

....

....

....

*I consider that our present sufferings are not worth
comparing with the glory that will be revealed in us.*
ROMANS 8:18 NIV

Joy of Heaven

When the world beats you down, look up. The heavens declare the glory of the Lord. You can find Me in blue skies with white fluffy clouds. You sense that I am near when you gaze into the night sky, each star hung in its place with perfection.

It was necessary that I die for your sins. It was God's plan because sin cannot enter into His glorious presence, and He wanted you to know the joy of heaven.

I am preparing a place for you in glory. I would not lie to you. I long for the day when I can return for you. Until then, look up.

....

....

....

....

....

....

....

....

....

....

"My Father's house has many rooms; if that were not so, would I have told you that I am going there to prepare a place for you? And if I go and prepare a place for you, I will come back and take you to be with me that you also may be where I am. You know the way to the place where I am going."
JOHN 14:2–4 NIV

Stay the Course

Work can be discouraging. You may feel as if you are stuck doing a meaningless task day in and day out. You may wonder why I would choose to leave you there and not put you in another position.

Remember that every day you are doing the work that is set before you. You are in this position for a reason. You will encounter people you can share the Gospel with, people who need encouragement, and those who need to sense My love. You can love the people you work with and those who pass through your workplace in a unique manner, because you are you.

As a Christian, you are not just working for an earthly supervisor—you are working for Me. Give your best always. Stay the course. I will reward you in the end.

....

....

....

....

....

....

....

In all the work you are doing, work the best you can. Work as if you were doing it for the Lord, not for people. Remember that you will receive your reward from the Lord, which he promised to his people. You are serving the Lord Christ.
Colossians 3:23–24 ncv

Draw Close

I have never sinned, but I fully understand temptation. I am completely God and yet I was also entirely man. I walked on earth for thirty-three years. It was not an easy journey from the manger to the cross, child. I know about exhaustion and discouragement. I know about disappointment and loss.

You can come to Me at any time, day or night. I am always here to listen, and it is with empathy, rather than just sympathy, that I am able to comfort you.

Instead of turning to others or to worldly pleasures to distract or numb your pain, draw close to Me. I have been there, and I will help you.

....

....

....

....

....

....

....

....

....

....

Since we have a great high priest, Jesus the Son of God, who has gone into heaven, let us hold on to the faith we have. For our high priest is able to understand our weaknesses. He was tempted in every way that we are, but he did not sin.
HEBREWS 4:14–15 NCV

Come Boldly

When you come to Me for help, come boldly. You are My precious one. I have saved you from darkness and brought you out into the light. I want nothing more than to provide the grace, mercy, and strength that you need today.

You do not have to hang your head in shame. My blood at Calvary covered that shame. When I look at you, I see righteousness. I purchased that righteousness for you. I paid a heavy price on the cross. Do you remember My words? "It is finished." Your sin has been dealt with. You are Mine for all time.

So come confidently to your Redeemer. Run into My arms. Linger in My presence. Sit at the foot of My throne and rest your weary head upon My lap. I will wipe the tears from your eyes. I will give you courage and help.

....

....

....

....

....

....

....

....

Let us then approach God's throne of grace with confidence, so that we may receive mercy and find grace to help us in our time of need.
HEBREWS 4:16 NIV

Rest in the Promise

I can see that you are hurting, child. Even when those around you believe that your smile is real, I know what is really going on in your heart. I sense your fear of the future. I am there when you toss and turn with worry throughout the night.

You are more important to Me than anything else in all of creation. Mankind is My pride and joy, My masterpiece, My best work! When I made man, I breathed life into him. I created you in My image.

I am not a negligent father. I am constantly and carefully watching over you. I know the number of hairs on your head. I don't miss a beat. I have promised never to leave you. Rest in that promise today.

"Are not two sparrows sold for a penny? Yet not one of them will fall to the ground outside your Father's care. And even the very hairs of your head are all numbered. So don't be afraid; you are worth more than many sparrows."
MATTHEW 10:29–31 NIV

A Mustard Seed

A father brought his son to Me. The son had an unclean spirit that was causing him to experience horrible convulsions. This was a lifelong burden. It had been happening since the boy's childhood.

When that spirit came into My presence, it went wild. The young man thrashed about uncontrollably. It was truly a horrific scene. I asked his father if he believed. His answer may remind you of your own faith. He said, "Lord, I believe," and these words were followed immediately with, "Help my unbelief!"

This man had faith like a mustard seed. He wanted to believe that I would save his son. He knew I was able.

In that instant, I commanded the spirit to come out and never enter the man's son again. The convulsions stopped. His life was changed forever.

What is your lifelong struggle? Give it to Me today. It just takes faith the size of a mustard seed.

....

....

....

....

....

....

....

....

*Immediately the father of the child cried out and
said with tears, "Lord, I believe; help my unbelief!"*
MARK 9:24 NKJV

What is your lifelong struggle? Give it to Me today. It just takes faith the size of a mustard seed.

Always Hope

Consider today what you are not. You may be discouraged, but you are not destroyed. You may be down, but you are not devastated. There is always hope in My name. There is always a second chance, a new start, a clean slate.

You will have trouble in this world. Since humankind chose to sin in the Garden of Eden, the world has not been as it was intended. You are tossed about and affected daily by your sins and the sins of others. It is a rough ride, at times a bumpy journey.

Today I want you to realize that this is not the end of your story. This is not the giving-up point. This is the getting-up point. I am here with My hand extended to help you. Let's begin again.

We are pressed on every side by troubles, but we are not crushed. We are perplexed, but not driven to despair. We are hunted down, but never abandoned by God. We get knocked down, but we are not destroyed.
2 Corinthians 4:8–9 nlt

Hiding Place

The world has you so busy, working day and night. Come away with Me to replenish your soul. I am your almighty God, sovereign over all things. I am your hiding place.

Steal away. Come and abide with Me. Set aside time to rest in the shadow of My protective wing. Allow Me to be your refuge. Allow Me to give you rest. I am all the protection you need. I will sustain you, rejuvenate you, and set you on course again.

When your mind races a hundred miles an hour and the world pulls you this way and that, learn to stop. Learn to say no to some things so that you can answer My call. I call you to sit awhile. Lean into Me. Trust Me. I am always going to be here for you. No one else can make you that promise.

....

....

....

....

....

....

....

....

....

He who dwells in the secret place of the Most High
shall abide under the shadow of the Almighty.
PSALM 91:1 NKJV

Strong

I protect you. I am your Refuge and your Fortress. When the battle rages outside, you are safe with Me. I will protect you more than the savings in your bank account or the walls you build ever could. These are material things—here today and gone tomorrow. I am your Savior, Redeemer, and Friend. I never change.

As long as you are living in the world, there will always be a battle for your attention. The world will call to you, tempting you with fleshly desires. You have been sealed with the Holy Spirit—He is fighting for you also. You will be torn between the spirit and the flesh all of your days.

Allow Me to be your refuge from the storm. Come to Me when you are weak, child, for I am strong. I long to be your Fortress, your Strong Tower, your Deliverance.

....

....

....

....

....

....

....

....

....

I will say of the LORD, "He is my refuge and
my fortress; my God, in Him I will trust."
PSALM 91:2 NKJV

Redeemer

Lay down your sordid past. I will restore to you the months and years you feel you wasted. Nothing is wasted in My economy. See, I have used that pain and those mistakes in your life. Are you wiser now? Do you see that My way is the only way that brings true delight? Are you able to help others who are hurting? Then those years, no matter how awful they may have been, were not in vain.

Look right into My glory. I am far, far greater than your worst mistake. I am the Redeemer. It is My purpose and My joy to take that which hurts you, that which drags you down, and use it for your good.

I have salvaged your messy past. You have a new name. I want you to walk in the victory of My forgiveness, not in the shadows of your past. Not even one more step.

....

....

....

....

....

....

....

....

And I will restore to you the years that the locust hath eaten,
the cankerworm, and the caterpiller, and the palmerworm,
my great army which I sent among you.
JOEL 2:25 KJV

Just as I led the Israelites
in a pillar of cloud by day,
I will lead you. Take My hand.
Let's do this day together.

Together

I am with you day and night, child. When the sun comes up in the morning, I am thinking of you. I set before you another day of life, another opportunity for you to walk with Me and talk with Me, another twenty-four hours for you to be My witness in a lost world.

Are you thinking of Me? Do you start your day with Me? Much of your dismay and discontent could be turned to stability and joy if only you would start your mornings in My presence.

Before you hurry into the demands of the day, stop and spend some time with your Savior. I want to meet with you and guide you throughout the day. Just as I led the Israelites in a pillar of cloud by day, I will lead you. Take My hand. Let's do this day together.

....

....

....

....

....

....

....

....

....

....

And the Lord went before them by day in a pillar of cloud
to lead the way, and by night in a pillar of fire to give
them light, so as to go by day and night.
EXODUS 13:21 NKJV

The Light

Life is made up of seasons. Just as winter gives way to the warmth of springtime, so your sadness will be replaced once more with laughter. The tides roll in and invade the peaceful shore, but without fail, they move back out into the ocean's depths.

When grief and loneliness overwhelm you, hold on. Come to Me in prayer. Spend time soaking up My Word. Dwell on the promises I have made to you. I have promised you a hope and a future. I have promised never to leave you. I am always watching over your life. My promises are yours to claim in every season, no matter how bad you feel.

This too shall pass.

I have not promised you a trouble-free life, but you will experience mountaintops along with the valleys where sorrow brings you low. In this season of darkness, keep your eyes on the light. Joy shall be yours again in due time.

....

....

....

....

....

....

....

....

For His anger is but for a moment, His favor is for life;
weeping may endure for a night, but joy comes in the morning.
Psalm 30:5 nkjv

Perfect Love

Think about how much I love you.

I came to earth to be born as a baby, laid in an animal's food trough for My bed. I lived as a man without a home. My dusty feet were tired day after day from ministry journeys. I was followed by people who all wanted something from Me—healing, miracles, and answers.

I, who never committed a sin, died a criminal's death on the cross. They hung a sign over My head and called out, "King of the Jews! Come down and save Yourself!" But I did not come down. I stayed there and I died. I did this out of My deep love for all mankind.

My love is far greater than any earthly love. I died for you to fulfill God's plan. I went to the cross so that you did not have to. Rest in My perfect love today. I will never leave you—not even for one moment.

....

....

....

....

....

....

....

....

....

....

There is no fear in love. But perfect love drives out fear, because fear has to do with punishment. The one who fears is not made perfect in love.
1 John 4:18 niv

Nothing Has Changed

Today you are distraught. You are not alone in feeling that way. Men and women of faith have experienced sadness and distress throughout the ages. Take heart—they have also experienced My faithfulness. I never neglect My children. I am with you wherever you go.

Erect altars within your heart, child. Put down a stake in those places where I have come through for you. They are many. On your low days, remember the mountaintops. Remember that I answer prayers. Sometimes I may seem slow to answer. I may allow you to linger for a while in a place that seems less than desirable to you. There is always a reason.

Look back. Do you see those altars? Do you remember those times I was faithful? Nothing has changed. I am still walking with you day by day.

....

....

....

....

....

....

....

....

....

....

"Then come, let us go up to Bethel, where I will build an altar to God, who answered me in the day of my distress and who has been with me wherever I have gone."
GENESIS 35:3 NIV

I Am Bigger

Anguish. It is a depth of sorrow that I see daily as My eyes move back and forth across the earth. Were it not for the Fall, it would not be so. There was no sorrow in Eden. There was perfection there, for a time, before mankind rebelled against God and sin came into the world.

But now there is sorrow. My people cry. They hurt. They are mistreated and rejected. People let other people down. Sin stings, and anger and rebellion run rampant. Yes, now there is anguish.

In your moments of anguish, allow Me to intervene. Remember that I am bigger than the tough situations you face. I can fill the empty places in your heart. I can relieve the grief. I have sent the Spirit to comfort and counsel you.

In your anguish, you are not abandoned. You are still here, close to My side, closer even on your sad days than you can imagine. I bind up the wounds of the brokenhearted. I am near.

*In her deep anguish Hannah prayed to the L*ORD*, weeping bitterly.*
1 Samuel 1:10 niv

Wise

When you are hurting, it is easy to lash out at those around you. This is a reaction that comes from your flesh. You are human—that is a fact, dear one, but not an excuse. You have been given the Holy Spirit. Call upon Him.

When you sense that you are going to lose your temper, ask the Spirit to calm you. Hold your tongue; you will be thankful later that you did. If you let it have free rein, you will end up cleaning up mess after mess. It is impossible to take back a spoken word. Remember this: words spoken in anger can remain in another's heart for a lifetime.

When you want to attack others, remember that many times the root of your hurt has nothing to do with them. Be wise. Control your temper. When you are hurting, cast your cares at My feet. Tell Me all about it. We will work through it together.

....

....

....

....

....

....

....

....

....

....

Foolish people lose their tempers, but wise people control theirs.
PROVERBS 29:11 NCV

In Peace

I am so sorry you are hurting. I know you have cried more tears than anyone should have to cry. I did not like the wrong that was done to you. Whatever hurts My children hurts My heart as well.

In your hurt, do not seek revenge. Revenge never satisfies, but instead only complicates things further. The best way to achieve peace is to let go of your hurt. Allow time and My love to heal your broken heart.

Everyone must one day stand before Me for what she or he has done in this life. Leave the judgment to Me. I will discipline when necessary. I will punish and strike down where I see fit. This is not for you to dictate or control. Do all that you can to walk in peace with those around you, and leave the vengeance to Me.

....

....

....

....

....

....

....

....

....

....

*My friends, do not try to punish others when they wrong you,
but wait for God to punish them with his anger. It is written:
"I will punish those who do wrong; I will repay them," says the Lord.*
ROMANS 12:19 NCV

I am already your Savior.
I long to be your closest
Friend as well.

Closest Friend

I want to be part of your daily life. I am not a king who desires to keep his distance in a palace, ruling over his subjects but never knowing their names and faces. I want to walk and talk with you. I want to be more like family than a houseguest.

Perhaps you invited Me into your heart long ago, but you have left Me alone in the foyer while you roam about in all the other rooms and nooks and crannies. May I come in farther, past the niceties and greeting at the door? Shall we become a bit less formal, you and I? Today would be a great day to spend some time fellowshipping together, just chatting about all that is going on in your life. I am already your Savior. I long to be your closest Friend as well.

....

....

....

....

....

....

....

....

....

....

"Look! I stand at the door and knock. If you hear my
voice and open the door, I will come in, and we
will share a meal together as friends."
REVELATION 3:20 NLT

Stand firm in your faith
today. Worship even
through your pain.

You Are Blessed

Job was tested and tried perhaps more than any other believer who has ever lived. He lost his family and all that was dear to him. He was afflicted in so many ways, and yet he would not curse God. He recognized that every gift comes down from heaven. He also acknowledged that it is God who gives and takes away.

Whether you feel blessed today or not, you are. You have received the gift of salvation and eternal life with Me. One day all the struggles that you face on earth will be forgotten. Stand firm in your faith today. Worship even through your pain.

....

....

....

....

....

....

....

....

....

....

Job stood up and tore his robe in grief. Then he shaved his head and fell to the ground to worship. He said, "I came naked from my mother's womb, and I will be naked when I leave. The LORD gave me what I had, and the LORD has taken it away. Praise the name of the LORD!"
JOB 1:20–21 NLT

Fellowship

Even when you are not at your very best, you can be an encouragement to those around you. No matter your mood, you can still smile. You can still offer a greeting to someone. You can ask how they are doing, and you can listen to what they say.

Don't give up meeting with other Christians. Believers need one another. You need your brothers and sisters, and likewise, they need you. You are living in difficult days. As the days grow even darker, instead of isolating yourself, draw near and fellowship with those who are like-minded in the faith. Lift others up, and allow others to be a light to you as well.

....

....

....

....

....

....

....

....

....

....

Let us think of ways to motivate one another to acts of love and good works. And let us not neglect our meeting together, as some people do, but encourage one another, especially now that the day of his return is drawing near.
HEBREWS 10:24–25 NLT

In the Valley

You are My precious child and I hate to see you worry. Worry puts a frown on your face. It steals your joy and eats up your days.

I long to see your light countenance and bright eyes that again trust Me for a bright future. I have given you each day as a gift, and I long to see you basking in its glory rather than filling it with anxious thoughts that do no good. Still, I know you are human. I know the world has dealt you many stresses.

There are mountaintop moments in life, certainly, but on the days when you are in the valley, you cannot feel any lower. For now, you must face these trials, but know that I am in control. One day I will take them all away. I will not let disappointment doom you. I am here even in the midst of the storm. Be encouraged. Stand firm in your faith. I love you.

Worry weighs a person down;
an encouraging word cheers a person up.
Proverbs 12:25 nlt

Never Let Go

Never give up. You are not a child of the world. You are My child, purchased by My blood, which I shed willingly for you on Calvary. You are more than a conqueror, because you have been given a new name.

You cannot work to buy My favor or do enough good to outweigh even one tiny sin that would keep you from entering the presence of a holy God. That was My work, My task, My sacrifice to make. Not yours.

Never give up on your faith in Me to see you through. Never wonder if I have changed, if I have left you, or if I am unable to forgive you once again. I am the same yesterday, today, and tomorrow. I have promised never to abandon you. My grace abounds in your life. I am always on your side. Never let go of My hand. I've got you.

....

....

....

....

....

....

....

....

....

....

So I gave up in despair, questioning the
value of all my hard work in this world.
ECCLESIASTES 2:20 NLT

My grace abounds in
your life. I am always
on your side. Never let go
of My hand. I've got you.

Looking Outward

Self-absorption hurts you, child. I am not sure you realize this. When you look at your own circumstances long enough, you become consumed with them. Your focus on others allows you to get outside of your own situation. Do you know someone who is hurting today? Is there someone who is sick? Could you minister to anyone?

When you examine others' lives, you will no doubt find that they are in need as well. You may think of your trial as the hardest one, but everyone around you is also fighting a battle.

Reach out. Look for an opportunity to love another person today. With selflessness comes great blessing. Teach your spirit to avoid jealousy. Train your mind to recognize that everyone around you has a wound; no one has a perfect life. It is the human condition. Receive the blessing of looking outward today.

But if you are bitterly jealous and there is selfish ambition in your heart, don't cover up the truth with boasting and lying.
JAMES 3:14 NLT

Call Out

Do you remember the story of Daniel's three friends who were thrown into the fiery furnace? King Nebuchadnezzar was shocked when these young men claimed that even if their God did not save them, they would still praise Him. They knew He would. This is the God you serve, child.

You do not serve a lowercase *g* god. You serve the one true God, the Creator of the universe. I am His beloved Son. You are saved by your faith in My death for you on the cross. Call out to Me when you are afraid. When you face trials of many kinds, rest assured that you will never be abandoned.

....

....

....

....

....

....

....

....

....

"If we are thrown into the blazing furnace, the God we serve is able to deliver us from it, and he will deliver us from Your Majesty's hand. But even if he does not, we want you to know, Your Majesty, that we will not serve your gods or worship the image of gold you have set up."
DANIEL 3:17–18 NIV

I'll Carry You

As a child, you sang the song that said: *"Jesus loves me, this I know, for the Bible tells me so."*

You knew the words well. You sang: *"I am weak, but He is strong."* The words of that song are from scripture, and they are true. When you are at your weakest, when you think you cannot take one more step, My strength kicks in. I walk with you and even carry you when necessary.

Look to Me in times of sorrow and days of despair. There is no place I would rather be than with you. There is nothing I would rather do than help you. I will always come running. I am never far from you. In your brokenness, I can make you whole again. In your grief, I can provide joy. Let Me be your strength today. I love you, child.

....

....

....

....

....

....

....

....

....

....

And He said to me, "My grace is sufficient for you, for My strength is made perfect in weakness." Therefore most gladly I will rather boast in my infirmities, that the power of Christ may rest upon me.
2 Corinthians 12:9 nkjv

After God's Own Heart

David was called "a man after God's own heart," but he was not perfect. He sinned and fell short of the glory of God, just as every man who has ever lived. Yet he loved God. He knew where to turn when he had sinned. He knew the One to call on when he was distressed or oppressed. He had faith and knew God would hear his prayers.

Cry out to Me when you are anxious and afraid. Fear is unavoidable—it is part of your human makeup. Still, it is not where you have to stay. You do not need to camp there in that fearful mindset, residing among your worries and anxieties. Seek Me and I will be easily found. I will deliver you, child, from everything that frightens you. Turn your cares over to the One who died to give you abundant life. Relinquish them today.

I sought the LORD, and He heard me,
and delivered me from all my fears.
PSALM 34:4 NKJV

Savior and Deliverer

As a Christian, you will face trials and tribulations that others may not. You will have to be strong in order to withstand temptations. The world will call to you, offering you pleasures that will only lead to destruction. Listen instead to My calling. I will never lead you astray, child.

You may face persecution from those who do not understand your choices and your dedication to My ways and My precepts. Know that you are not left to fend for yourself. You do not have to worry about fighting or standing up for yourself. I will do that for you.

Just as the shepherd rejoices over finding his one lost little sheep, I hold each of My children dear to My heart. I see your faithfulness and I see your struggles. I will never give you more than you can bear. I am your Savior and your Deliverer. Trust always in Me.

....
....
....
....
....
....
....
....
....

Many are the afflictions of the righteous,
but the LORD delivers him out of them all.
PSALM 34:19 NKJV

I am your Savior
and your Deliverer.
Trust always in Me.

Good and Perfect Gift

I died for you on the cross. I was put to death by crucifixion, the most painful, horrible death of all. It was the death reserved for criminals. I was laughed at and mocked. I was offered bitter vinegar to drink. A sign was hung above My head that said KING OF THE JEWS. It was their version of a joke. They hated Me.

God could have chosen to let that cup pass from Me. Instead, He loved mankind enough to watch Me die. Would a God like that withhold any good or perfect gift from His children?

Give thanks today in whatever circumstance you find yourself, even if you cannot sense or see God's hand. He is at work. He loved you enough to watch His only Son die on a cross for your sins. He is not a withholder. Trust in Him. Trust also in Me.

....
....
....
....
....
....
....
....
....
....

He who did not spare His own Son, but delivered Him up for us all,
how shall He not with Him also freely give us all things?
ROMANS 8:32 NKJV

Nothing Is Impossible

Do you find your thoughts constantly drifting to the negative? Is it hard for you not to obsess over your current struggle? Ask Me to help you control those thoughts. Take every thought captive in My holy name.

Instead of giving Me a certain segment of your day for prayer, try praying throughout your day. Dwell on My promises. Post them on your mirror and the refrigerator door, places where you're sure to see them throughout the day.

Keep truth always before you so that you do not buy in to the devil's lies. He wants nothing more than to convince you that you have no hope. He would love to keep your mind forever stayed upon lesser things. In Me, child, you have great hope. Every day is a new opportunity, and nothing is impossible with God.

....

....

....

....

....

....

....

....

....

And now, dear brothers and sisters, one final thing. Fix your thoughts on what is true, and honorable, and right, and pure, and lovely, and admirable. Think about things that are excellent and worthy of praise.
PHILIPPIANS 4:8 NLT

Never Alone

I go before you. I have set My angels around you. I also follow you. I am all around you, watching and keeping you from harm you do not even see. You may feel alone, but you truly never are. You need only look to Me.

I am your Prince of Peace. I am aware of another prince. He is the prince of darkness, and he would love to steal the joy I have put in your heart. Don't allow it. Remember that you belong to Me. Nothing can ever change that. You are sealed with My redemptive blood. You are saved. Eternal life is your gift from Me, and it begins by living an abundant life on the earth. I am with you always.

Let that be enough today. Let's face this together. I will not fail you, nor will I ever abandon you.

....

....

....

....

....

....

....

....

....

*"Do not be afraid or discouraged, for the LORD will
personally go ahead of you. He will be with you;
he will neither fail you nor abandon you."*
DEUTERONOMY 31:8 NLT

Freed

Depression has a way of taking you to a desert. You feel alone, even in the most beautiful place with great people all around you. Depression steals your joy. It weighs you down under the heaviest load. It strips you of light and leaves you instead with a sad darkness. I know, child. I see.

Seek the help I have put before you this day. Come to Me in prayer. Reach out to Christian friends around you. Seek assistance from medical professionals and counselors whom I have set in the world for this purpose.

Don't stay in the desert. There is so much help available for you. I want you to enjoy life. I want you to find happiness again. Reach up and reach out. It is time to be freed from the wasteland.

....
....
....
....
....
....
....
....
....
....
....

"He found them in a desert land, in an empty, howling wasteland.
He surrounded them and watched over them; he guarded
them as he would guard his own eyes."
DEUTERONOMY 32:10 NLT

I Will Come

Waiting is never easy. Trust Me, though, when I tell you I will always come to you. You may have to wait, but I will come. I may not always take away the trial, but I will carry you through it. I may not always answer your prayers just the way you want, but I will never fail to give you what you need. Allow Me to be the firm foundation of your life. Cry out to Me. In due time, I will lift you up. You will never wait even one moment too long. I am never early and I am never late.

Stand on the rock of your faith, and you will be prepared for any storm that comes your way, even if it blows up suddenly and takes you by surprise.

....

....

....

....

....

....

....

....

....

I waited patiently for the LORD; he turned to me and heard my cry.
He lifted me out of the slimy pit, out of the mud and mire; he set
my feet on a rock and gave me a firm place to stand.
PSALM 40:1–2 NIV

Allow Me to be the firm
foundation of your life.
Cry out to Me. In due time,
I will lift you up.

Your Song

Have you lost your song? Where once there was joy and peace in your life, are you now downcast?

I want to give you your song back. In fact, I want to give you a new song. When you begin to praise Me, your heart will change. It may not be sudden, but as you sing, day by day, things will begin to look brighter.

Worship Me, child. Look to Me. Lean into Me. I have not turned away. I am still here. I am the One you trusted in before, and I am still found faithful.

When you have lost the music in your life, I will hum along with you until you can remember. I will give you new lyrics. I will compose a new love song in your heart. I cherish you. Trust in Me today, and sing a new song.

....
....
....
....
....
....
....
....
....
....

He put a new song in my mouth, a hymn of praise to our God.
Many will see and fear the LORD and put their trust in him.
PSALM 40:3 NIV

Love

Are you doubting My love for you?

Remember the cross. I served as a perfect sacrifice for your sin, and you were not even born yet. I loved you in your rebellion as a sinner. I loved you then, and I love you still. I went to the cross once and for all. It was a payment for sin, and it was offered to you as a free gift.

Because I am your Savior, you are seen as righteous by the Father. He sees you through a lens that bears My name. . .and My scars. Can you believe, child, that I could not love you one ounce more if I tried? I love you with all of My heart.

....

....

....

....

....

....

....

....

....

....

But he was pierced for our rebellion, crushed for our sins. He was beaten so we could be whole. He was whipped so we could be healed. All of us, like sheep, have strayed away. We have left God's paths to follow our own. Yet the LORD laid on him the sins of us all.
ISAIAH 53:5–6 NLT

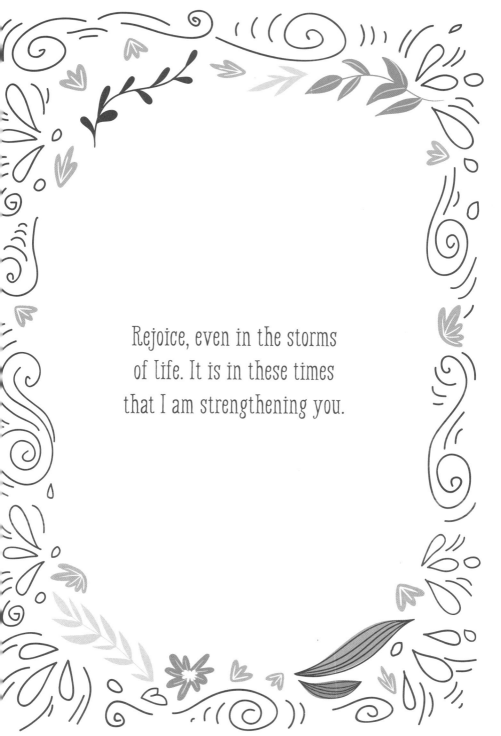

Rejoice, even in the storms
of life. It is in these times
that I am strengthening you.

Endurance

Have you heard about the tiny sea turtles that, when hatched, must make their way across the seashore to the ocean? If a person picks them up and helps them out, they will die. Do you know why? It is in their struggle through the sand that their little flippers are strengthened. Meaning well, the human provides an easier transit—a ride, if you will. But removing the struggle actually proves detrimental to the turtle. Without strong flippers, they cannot swim. The waves overtake them and they cannot survive.

The same is true for you. If you lived a trouble-free life, you would never grow stronger in your faith walk. You would not develop endurance. You would be weak where you need to be strong. Trust Me in your trials. Rejoice, even in the storms of life. It is in these times that I am strengthening you.

....

....

....

....

....

....

....

....

....

....

We can rejoice, too, when we run into problems and trials,
for we know that they help us develop endurance.
ROMANS 5:3 NLT

Perfect Timing

Isn't it wonderful when you can see My hand in your life? Do you smile and note that My timing was perfect? Child, you can trust that it is always so.

I was sent into the world at just the right time to save it. At just the right time in history, I was nailed to a cross to die for all mankind. All those who call upon My name are saved because of that act. God carried out His plan to bring you into a right relationship with Him.

And so today, in whatever difficult circumstance you are experiencing, know that My timing never fails. I will continue to show up in your life with just the right answer at just the right time. It may not always be the timing you would choose, but I always choose what I know to be best for My own.

When we were utterly helpless, Christ came
at just the right time and died for us sinners.
ROMANS 5:6 NLT

Be Kind

Have your feelings been hurt? Has your heart been wounded by the words or actions of another? This is so common in the fallen world in which you live. It happens every day. Sometimes the result is bitterness and dissension, the parting of ways, the ending of a friendship, or divorce. Other times you can choose forgiveness. It is an act of sheer will. It goes against your humanity. It is only accomplished through the Holy Spirit, whom I sent into the world to counsel you.

Be kind. Choose to lavish grace upon others. Just as you have been so often forgiven, forgive those who offend you. It is no fun to feel hurt or rejected. It stings and aches and can consume you, but only if you let it. The choice is yours. I hope you will find a way to forgive. Forgiveness provides the pathway to freedom from your wounds.

....

....

....

....

....

....

....

....

....

....

And be kind to one another, tenderhearted,
forgiving one another, even as God in Christ forgave you.
Ephesians 4:32 nkjv

Be Still

When you think of a fight, what images come to mind? Do you imagine arms flailing and fists pounding? I want you to know that this is not the only way to fight. If you will just be still, I will fight on your behalf.

Do you remember the story of the Israelites crossing the Red Sea? God parted the waters and saw them through, and then what happened? He destroyed the Egyptians. Not one of them walked across. They were caught up in the waters and put to death. Not just part of Pharaoh's army, but every last soldier. Not just the people, but the horses as well. If the world had been looking on just a few minutes prior to this great miracle, it would have thought the Israelites did not have a chance. With God, they had every chance!

Let Me fight your battles. I have redeemed you from sin, and I stand ready to fight on your behalf.

....

....

....

....

....

....

....

....

....

....

"The Lord will fight for you while you keep silent."
Exodus 14:14 nasb

Allow Me. . .

It is tempting to take matters into your own hands when someone wrongs you. This is not your job. Instead, seek to live at peace with everyone with whom you possibly can. Allow Me to take care of those who hurt you.

Rest assured that no one benefits from hurting you. I am able to take that which others mean for evil and use it for good in your life. I know that unfair words and actions sting. It feels horrible to be abandoned or rejected by someone you trusted. This is a fallen world and people are capable of great evil. Do not bear the burden of revenge. It is not pleasant and it never comes out well. Allow Me to handle the people who come against you. Leave that up to Me.

Never take your own revenge, beloved, but leave room for the wrath of God, for it is written, "Vengeance is Mine, I will repay," says the Lord.
Romans 12:19 nasb

Bring your requests before Me.
Listen to Me. Linger for a
while in My presence.

Heart Focus

Never feel that you must come to Me with perfect words. You don't even have to come with words at all. I just want you to come to Me in prayer. I am looking for your heart to be focused on Me. I want to know that you recognize that every good gift comes from above.

I am not concerned with the language you use. I am not interested in prayers that you recite or how long your prayers are. Anyone can stand before others and call out a beautiful-sounding prayer. I am interested in *you*. You are My precious one, and I long to communicate with you.

Bring your requests before Me. Listen to Me. Linger for a while in My presence. I love you so much, child.

....

....

....

....

....

....

....

....

....

....

"And when you are praying, do not use meaningless
repetition as the Gentiles do, for they suppose that
they will be heard for their many words."
MATTHEW 6:7 NASB

Mine

You may be sorrowful, but you will not be swallowed up. You may feel discouraged, but you have not been discarded. I am the Light of the world, and I shine brightest when you find yourself in dark circumstances. I bind up the wounds of the brokenhearted. I am always near.

You will face enemies in life. They may be those who do not understand your convictions or your ways. You are in the world, but you are not of it. You are an alien there, for heaven is your true home.

As you journey through life, remember that you are not alone. When you fall, I will always help you up again. I will set your feet on a solid path. I will not allow you to be brought down by the evil one. You are Mine.

....
....
....
....
....
....
....
....
....
....

Do not rejoice over me, O my enemy. Though I fall I will rise;
though I dwell in darkness, the LORD is a light for me.
MICAH 7:8 NASB

Start Today

I know what you need before you even ask. I see your heart and feel your longings. I am omnipresent and omniscient. I am everywhere and I know everything.

This doesn't mean that your prayers do not affect Me. I long to hear your requests. I love it when you come to Me and share your praises and concerns. Even though I know your needs, it means a lot to Me for you to express them to Me. This shows Me that you recognize I am your Provider and your Good Shepherd.

I am here to lead and guide you. I love to answer your prayers. Prayer affects you too. As you pray and as you see prayers answered in your life, you will grow in your faith. This is one of the many benefits of prayer. Make it a priority. Start today.

....

....

....

....

....

....

....

....

....

....

"So do not be like them; for your Father
knows what you need before you ask Him."
MATTHEW 6:8 NASB

Live fully today.
Experience the abundant
life that I came to give you.

Live Fully

I want you to have abundant life. That is why I came to earth.

I was born in a manger and lived a human life. I was fully man and yet also fully God. It is a mystery that you must have faith to believe, but it is true. I went to the cross. I allowed Myself to be crucified there, tortured, mocked, put to death. I died to give you life. The gift of eternal life does not begin when you die, child. It has already begun.

Each day is a gift. I know that you are hurting. I know that you wish your situation was a bit different today. You don't see all of the good plans I have for you. You see only the present. I am in charge of your future, and it is bright.

Live fully today. Experience the abundant life that I came to give you.

·····

·····

·····

·····

·····

·····

·····

·····

·····

·····

"A thief comes to steal and kill and destroy,
but I came to give life—life in all its fullness."
JOHN 10:10 NCV

True Peace

The world will try to offer you peace. Satan will whisper his lies to you, tempting you to do things that are outside of My will for you. He will try to convince you this is the road to peace, but it isn't. True peace comes only through your relationship with Me.

In the midst of horrible circumstances, My people can find peace. Whether you have been abandoned by a spouse or are without a job, you can be at peace. You can find peace in Me when you feel alone or sad. You can be at peace when others come against you unfairly.

Call out to Me. I am the One who walked on water, the One who calmed the storm with My command. Don't be shocked at My power. You know Me. I am Jesus, Son of the Living God. I am your Savior and Redeemer and Friend. I alone can give you peace. Accept it as a free gift today.

God is not a God of confusion but a God of peace.
1 Corinthians 14:33 ncv

Precious One

When I saved you, I went down into the pit. I did not just toss you a rope and tell you to hang on tight while I lifted you. I came for you. I came *all the way down into the filthy mire of your sin*. I went to the depths of the pit, and I rescued you.

When you feel all alone, call out to Me. When you are depressed, I am still here loving you. When you feel like you can't go on, when it feels like sorrow will swallow you whole, cry out My name. I will always come to your aid.

I may allow trials and struggles in your life, and I know you cannot comprehend this. But I will never leave you in the pit. You are My precious one. Remember this. Call on Me. I will come.

....
....
....
....
....
....
....
....
....
....
....

I called on your name, LORD, from the depths of the pit.
LAMENTATIONS 3:55 NIV

Brighter Days

Life is full of mountains and valleys. Perhaps right now you find yourself in a season of deep loss and grief. You may have lost someone through death, divorce, rejection, or abandonment.

Grief is a heavy price to pay for love, but you still pay it. When you find yourself in a place of deep sorrow, hold on. Know that I am with you and that around the corner there will be a spot of sunlight. The pain will subside. You will always feel the loss, but it will not always be as unbearable as it seems at this moment. Grief will give way to joy. My compassion will not allow you to stay in this place of mourning all of your life.

Walk with Me. Trust in Me. Brighter days are just ahead.

....

....

....

....

....

....

....

....

....

Though he brings grief, he will show compassion,
so great is his unfailing love. For he does not
willingly bring affliction or grief to anyone.
Lamentations 3:32–33 niv

Do Not Fear

Just as a mother comforts her child when he awakens after a bad dream, I am here to calm your fears. I know that this world is a scary place. The shadows and noises in the night that frightened you as a child have given way to greater worries. As an adult, you may fear the future. Your finances may concern you deeply. How will you pay the bills? How can you keep from losing your home? You may also be worried about your relationships, your children, or your job.

Whatever you fear today, child, simply call out to Me. I am near to those whose hearts are troubled. I tell you, "Do not fear." I am able to do above and beyond what you could ever imagine. Nothing is impossible with Me. So take My hand and dry your eyes. There is no need to fear the future. I hold it in My hands.

....

....

....

....

....

....

....

....

....

You came near when I called you, and you said, "Do not fear."
LAMENTATIONS 3:57 NIV

Trust in Me and seek Me daily.
I will bless you with peace
that passes all understanding.

One Thing at a Time

The world is a busy place. There are so many people, places, and problems fighting for your attention. You have demands at home and work, with family and friends. Does your mind seem to whirl sometimes? Step back and focus on just one thing at a time.

If you want to experience true peace, you must choose to put Me first, even with all the daily pressures of life. Carve out time to spend in My presence. Talk, but also listen. I want to lighten your load and lead you by still waters.

Trust in Me and seek Me daily. I will bless you with peace that passes all understanding. No matter what else is going on in your life, child, I always want to be your "one thing." Then everything else will fall into place as it should.

....

....

....

....

....

....

....

....

....

....

You will keep in perfect peace those whose
minds are steadfast, because they trust in you.
ISAIAH 26:3 NIV

A New Creation

Lawyers consider carefully whether or not to take a case. They contemplate the evidence, weighing the pros and cons. They try to determine whether they will be able to win. Not so with Me. I took up your case before you were even born. Before you were even a thought in your mother's mind, I was thinking of you. I was hanging on a cross giving My life for you. Your case had already been won. The verdict was in. Salvation. Eternal life. Abundant life. Redemption. Forgiveness of sin. Death, burial, but then. . .resurrection.

Your life has been redeemed. You are a new creation. Find within your heart the strength to give thanks today that I took up your case and saved your soul. I loved you that much. I love you the same today. My love will be with you all of your days, the good and the bad days alike.

You, Lord, took up my case; you redeemed my life.
Lamentations 3:58 niv

A Rock

Have you ever tried to walk through sand? It moves and shifts beneath your bare feet. To build a home upon the sand would be foolish, wouldn't it? Yet people attempt to construct their lives upon such a foundation every day. The world offers a lot of shifting sands for a foundation, but none can withstand the storms of life. This is why you placed your trust in Me as your Savior.

I am a Rock—stable, strong, and unchanging. I am called the Cornerstone. The cornerstone is essential to any structure. Every other stone in a building is set in reference to the cornerstone. It determines the position of the entire structure.

Have you made Me the cornerstone of your life? Am I the foundation? If you will stand upon the Rock of your salvation and place your faith in Me, you will never be shaken. Regardless of the tough times that come your way, you will stand secure.

So, trust the Lord always, because he is our Rock forever.
Isaiah 26:4 ncv

Humility

Has your pride been hurt? Pray for those who have hurt you. The more you pray for them, the softer your heart will become toward them.

Humble yourself before Me. I am not suggesting that you do something I have not done Myself. I was ridiculed and mocked. People did not believe I was who I said I was. Even though I came to save them and I never committed one sin, I was chosen by the people to be crucified, while Barabbas was set free. They chose a criminal over Me.

I asked God to forgive them, for they did not know what they were doing as they nailed Me to the cross. So often when someone hurts you, it is the same. They are lashing out due to the hurt in their own hearts. They are insecure, so they tear you down in an attempt to build themselves up.

Humility is not always easy, but it always reaps great reward.

....

....

....

....

....

....

....

....

"God blesses those who are humble,
for they will inherit the whole earth."
MATTHEW 5:5 NLT

Humility is not
always easy, but it
always reaps great reward.

Justice

The world is not always just. In fact, it rarely is. You have probably been treated unfairly. If not, you will be. It is a fallen world you live in and your lifetime will be full of injustice.

You may bear scars of injustices inflicted upon you as a child. You may have been abused by a trusted adult in your life when you were young. You were afraid to tell the secrets for years to come. You may carry them to this day. Perhaps you have experienced injustices more recently in life—you have been left by a partner, rejected by a child, or passed over for a promotion in your work that you truly deserved.

One day there will be justice like you have never seen. In heaven, all things will be made right. There will be no more tears, pain, or injustice. Hold on, child. The day is coming. In the meantime, cast your cares upon Me. I am strong enough to bear the injustices that weigh you down.

*"God blesses those who hunger and thirst
for justice, for they will be satisfied."*
MATTHEW 5:6 NLT

The Right Thing

Have you been made fun of for choices you have made as a believer? Maybe you have been called a "goody-goody" for not taking part in an activity that you know does not honor Me.

A day is coming when you could experience persecution simply for saying you are a Christian. You may not have faced this yet, but it is likely to happen in your lifetime.

Doing the right thing does not always mean you'll be rewarded by the world. When you are honest, it does not always pay off automatically. When you are humble, someone may perceive you as weak and attempt to use or control you. Take heart. A day is coming when My Father promises to reward those who do right in a fantastic way. The kingdom of heaven will be yours!

Stand strong. Choose the right over the wrong. You will never regret it.

....

....

....

....

....

....

....

....

....

*"God blesses those who are persecuted for
doing right, for the Kingdom of Heaven is theirs."*
MATTHEW 5:10 NLT

A Time for Everything

Losing people you love is painful and difficult. You know you will see them again in heaven, and that should give you comfort. But in the meantime, it hurts. Nothing compares to the pain and sorrow associated with grief. It has the power to bring you very low. It is all-consuming and sometimes seems as if it will last forever.

The Bible says that there is a time for everything. There will unfortunately be times of mourning in your life. You will grieve over lost family members and friends. This is part of the human condition—you can't avoid it.

Find comfort in the fact that those who mourn are blessed. They are comforted. I sent the Holy Spirit into the world to comfort My own. This is His purpose, along with counseling you. Rest in the Holy Spirit and find peace, even in your days of mourning.

"Blessed are those who mourn, for they shall be comforted."
MATTHEW 5:4 NKJV

Rest in the Holy Spirit
and find peace, even in
your days of mourning.

Stand Strong

If you praise Me in the sunshine, don't question My goodness in the storms. I am good all the time. If you had no trials in life, your faith would never grow. You would not develop perseverance, which leads to strong character.

Consider the weather. Rain is a necessity—every day cannot be sunny. The same is true of your spirit. If pleasant days were all you ever knew, your spirit wouldn't grow in communion with Me.

My disciples suffered many hardships. They were called to leave their families and everything else behind to follow Me. The apostle Paul was imprisoned and shipwrecked. He did not have an easy life!

Accept the hard times, just as you accept the good, and praise My name. I know this isn't easy, but one day there will be no more hardships or hurts. For now, stand strong in your faith. I will see you through the dark days.

When life is good, enjoy it. But when life is hard, remember: God gives good times and hard times, and no one knows what tomorrow will bring.
ECCLESIASTES 7:14 NCV

Holiness

What are you lacking? What are you longing for? Come to Me and offer up your requests. Lay down your emptiness and ask to be filled again.

I see your needs before you speak them, but I still want you to seek My face. I want you to remember where the solutions to your problems are found—not in the world, but in Me. I will help you. I will never be one moment early, nor one second too late.

I want to fulfill your desires, but My greatest concern is for your holiness. Even above your happiness, I desire to see you become more like Me. I want you to grow in your dependence on Me. I want you to shine for Me even in the dark places where life takes you. Never wonder if you are on My mind. I want nothing but the very best for you.

....

....

....

....

....

....

....

....

....

....

But as for me, I am poor and needy; may the Lord think of me.
You are my help and my deliverer; you are my God, do not delay.
PSALM 40:17 NIV

Cleansing

Rain is cleansing. It is healing. It makes the trees and flowers grow. It refreshes people and animals. It fills lakes and rivers. Without it, crops dry up and drought comes upon the land. Rain is a blessing. Remember this, and thank Me for it.

Some people grumble about what they cannot do because the rains have come. Instead, try to find peace in the showers that I bring upon the earth. I speak to you not only through sunshine, but also through the rain.

Just as the rain brings a fresh start to the earth, I want to purify your heart. Let Me remove the bitterness that has built up there for so long. Allow Me to send My cool rains to wash away the dusty memories of all the hurt inflicted upon you. Be replenished by My Spirit. I love you, child. I want you to be refreshed so that you may experience joy again.

Ask the Lord for rain in the springtime; it is the Lord who sends the thunderstorms. He gives showers of rain to all people, and plants of the field to everyone.
Zechariah 10:1 niv

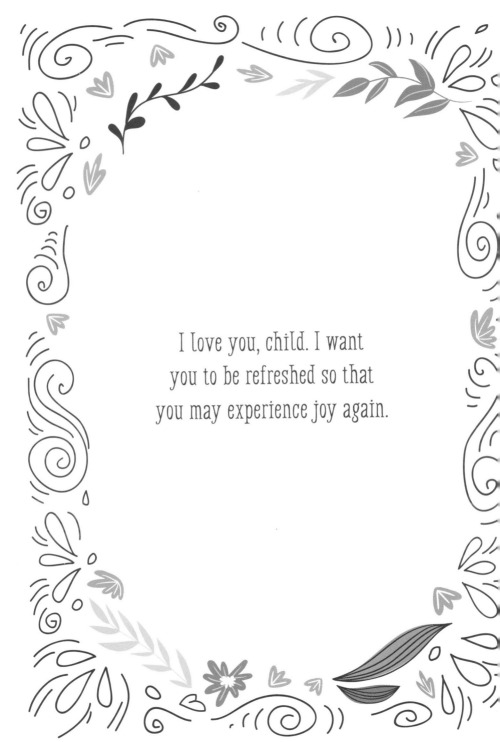

I love you, child. I want
you to be refreshed so that
you may experience joy again.

Remembered

Mankind is forgetful, but I am not. Just as God remembered Noah and all of his family and the animals on the ark, you are remembered also. You are made in the image of God. You are close to His heart.

The Father has given you to Me as a precious little sheep. I am your Good Shepherd. In an amazing way, sheep quickly learn the voice of their shepherd and are able to distinguish it from the voices of other shepherds. I am training you to hear My voice clearly, even though you will be called to by many others in your life. I will always lead you on the right path. I will never forget you. Dear one, even if you stray, hear My voice and come running back to Me. Do not forget the One who loves you most.

....

....

....

....

....

....

....

....

....

*But God remembered Noah and all the wild animals
and the livestock that were with him in the ark, and he
sent a wind over the earth, and the waters receded.*
GENESIS 8:1 NIV

Fresh Starts

If you read My Word, you will see clearly that there is a time for everything. There was a time, because of mankind's sin, for God to destroy the earth by a great flood. Then, after forty days of pouring rain, Noah was able to open a window he had made in the ark.

Have you been struggling, child? Do you wake up each day dreading the hours that stand between you and bedtime's return? Take heart. I will provide a window for you to open. You may need a little help to open it. It may be just a crack at first, just enough to let in a bit of light. But relief is on its way.

I am a God of second chances and fresh starts. I make a way where there seems to be none. I close doors, but after a time, I whisper that it is time to open a window.

_____

_____

_____

_____

_____

_____

_____

_____

_____

_____

After forty days Noah opened a window he had made in the ark.
GENESIS 8:6 NIV

Find Me in the sunshine and
the cool breeze. Know that
I have not left you, nor will
I ever. I love you, child.

Find Me...

I see you weeping today, just as I wept in the garden, asking God if the cup could pass. I see every tear. I know there is a deep sadness within your spirit.

I want you to know that I am proud of you. I see you put on a smile and continue to minister to others even on your hardest days. I see the way you care about people, even though you feel so downtrodden.

Brighter days are coming. Sorrow may last for a while, but My grace offers you abundant joy. My mercies, which are new every single morning, await you. Look for Me in the little things. While you wait for this burden to be lifted, find Me in the neighbor who reaches out to you. Find Me in the sunshine and the cool breeze. Know that I have not left you, nor will I ever. I love you, child.

....

....

....

....

....

....

....

....

....

Those who sow in tears shall reap in joy. He who continually goes forth weeping, bearing seed for sowing, shall doubtless come again with rejoicing, bringing his sheaves with him.
Psalm 126:5–6 nkjv

You Are Safe

I am gentle and slow to anger, but I am also mighty and powerful. The wind is at My command. I once commanded a storm to halt, and it subsided at the sound of My voice. My disciples couldn't believe it. I wondered why they were so surprised.

Do you know that everything that touches your life must first pass through My fingers, child? I am more powerful than Satan and all his schemes against you. I am mightier than the world that seeks to devour you. I am your Savior.

I did not save you from your sins only to throw you to the wolves. I watch over your comings and goings. I protect you and surround you with My angels.

Rest in Me today. Each day has enough worry of its own, and on this day I want you to choose to rest in My powerful but loving arms. I have you. You are safe.

....

....

....

....

....

....

....

....

Praise the LORD from the earth, you creatures of the ocean depths, fire and hail, snow and clouds, wind and weather that obey him.
PSALM 148:7–8 NLT

Child of the Light

Just as there are seasons throughout the year, there are seasons in your life.

In the wintertime, the trees are bare. The grass turns brown. Cold weather makes it hard for people to get out and be active. There is a purpose for winter, but aren't you glad to feel the warmth of the sun on those first spring days?

You may find yourself in a season of sorrow today, but just as winter gives way to spring, your sadness will give way to joy. Today you may not be able to imagine laughter and singing. Trust that I am at work. I will not leave you in mourning.

The veil will be lifted. I will not let you slip into the darkness. You are a child of the light. You are worth so much to Me!

For lo, the winter is past, the rain is over and gone. The flowers appear on the earth; the time of singing has come, and the voice of the turtledove is heard in our land.
Song of Solomon 2:11–12 nkjv

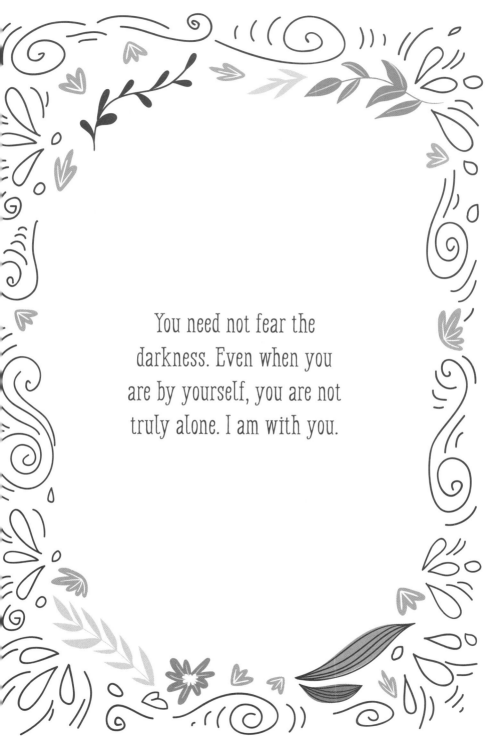

You need not fear the
darkness. Even when you
are by yourself, you are not
truly alone. I am with you.

Forever Safe

There is a spiritual battle going on all the time. I fight for you! The evil one would love nothing more than to bring you down because you are a believer. He wants to make you believe you are worthless and that you have no hope. Satan wants you to give in to depression and sorrow. He wants you to buy the lie that nothing will ever change and that you will never be happy again.

Satan can influence you if you let him, but your soul is forever safe with Me. You are not of his kingdom, because you are secure in Mine. You are not of this world, but you are in it for a time. You need not fear the darkness. Even when you are by yourself, you are not truly alone. I am with you.

....

....

....

....

....

....

....

....

....

....

So we say with confidence, "The Lord is my helper;
I will not be afraid. What can mere mortals do to me?"
HEBREWS 13:6 NIV

Your Helper

It is hard to ask for help. You are good at giving it, but it takes humility to ask for it. I am your Helper. I am always here. Ask Me to help you in the areas where you are lacking. Ask Me to provide what you need. I am ready to answer your prayers.

I have put other helpers in your life. Do you recognize them? Do you allow those in your life to reach out to you, or are you withdrawn and secluded? Have you built walls around your heart, too afraid to be vulnerable again? Child, I want to bless you through those I have put in your circles. Allow others to help you. You will grow from relationships with them. You may be able to help them in some way as well. Look around you for the helpers in your life.

....

....

....

....

....

....

....

....

....

....

The LORD is with me; he is my helper.
I look in triumph on my enemies.
PSALM 118:7 NIV

The More You Love

It is easy to pray for your loved ones, but it's a tall order to pray for your enemies. Yet this is My will for you, child. It will change your outlook. It may even change your life.

I prayed for those who persecuted Me. I called out to the Father on behalf of those who crucified Me. I instruct you to do the same. It is for your own good that I have asked this of you.

When you pray for those who have hurt you, your heart will learn to forgive them. Forgiveness is the only way that you can be truly free. When you pray for these people, your love for them will grow. The more you love, the less you will hurt.

Pray for those who hurt you. It is not always easy, but it is My way for you. Begin today.

....

....

....

....

....

....

....

....

....

....

"But I say to you, love your enemies. Pray for those who hurt you."
MATTHEW 5:44 NCV

Shine Brightly

I know that it is a mystery to you, but the Father and I are one. With the Holy Spirit, we make up the Trinity. We are separate and yet unified as one. I came to earth and lived among people. I was fully man and yet fully God. I came to make a way for mankind to be made right with God.

In Me there is no darkness. I am one with the Father and the Father is pure light. You are a child of the light. You are spending time in a dark world, but you can choose to shine for Me there. If you remain in the shadows, no one will know that you belong to Me. Shine brightly, child! Put off the hatred and dissension that the world promotes. Be filled instead with the fruit of the Spirit. My way is the way of light and love.

....

....

....

....

....

....

....

....

....

....

Here is the message we have heard from Christ and now announce to you: God is light, and in him there is no darkness at all.
1 John 1:5 ncv

All People

I know that someone has hurt you. It is hard for you to hear this, but I love that person dearly. I died that this person might have eternal life. Just as I came to die for your sins, I came to die for the sins of all mankind. It is My desire that all people will come to know Me.

Pray for those who hurt you and come against you. I call believers to live in peace. This does not mean that you have to be the best of friends again. You may have to set some boundaries or keep your distance from some people, but you can still pray for them. In time, you will even be able to offer forgiveness.

I do not like anything that hurts you, My precious one, but I love all mankind and I do not wish for anyone to perish in sin.

....

....

....

....

....

....

....

....

....

....

He died in our place to take away our sins,
and not only our sins but the sins of all people.
1 JOHN 2:2 NCV

Blessings of the Present

Just as Moses gave My message to the Israelites long ago, I am telling you this today: "You have been on this mountain long enough."

It was time for the Israelites to move on. They were to go into the Promised Land, the land that God was giving to them—a land flowing with milk and honey. I have such a land for you. It may not be a literal land, but I have a future for you that is bright and hopeful.

When you linger too long in the hurts of the past, you miss out on the blessings of the present and you can't look forward to the future. Break camp! It is time to leave lesser things behind. I want you to let go of the pain that causes bitterness to take root in your heart. I have good things in store for you.

....

....

....

....

....

....

....

....

....

....

"When we were at Mount Sinai, the LORD our God said to us, 'You have stayed at this mountain long enough. It is time to break camp and move on.'"
DEUTERONOMY 1:6–7 NLT

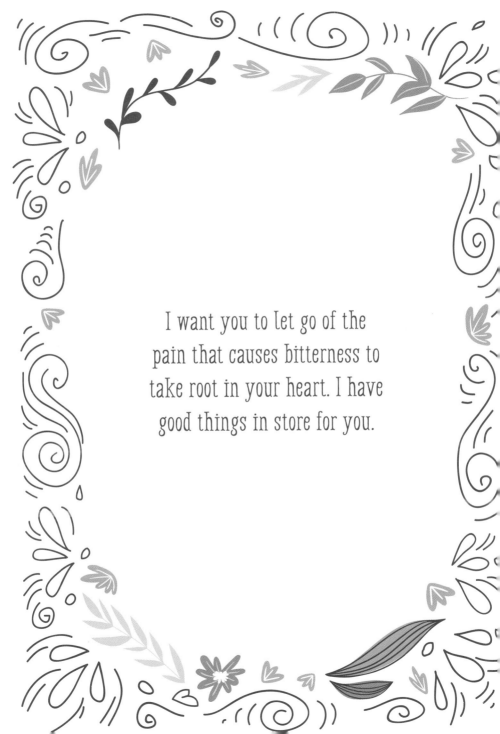

I want you to let go of the pain that causes bitterness to take root in your heart. I have good things in store for you.

I Cherish You

I know all about betrayal. I was betrayed by one of My followers, one of My chosen twelve disciples. It had to happen this way for God's plan to be fulfilled, but I was so sad when one so close turned against me. It happened for merely thirty pieces of silver. Was I not worth more than material wealth to him?

I know how it feels to have someone you trust let you down. I know it hurts. That hurt can cut deeper than most.

You trusted someone. You shared your heart with this person. You didn't expect betrayal. I know it came as a shock, and I am sorry you have had to experience it.

Know that even when others abandon you, I cherish you. What is meant for evil, I will use for good in your life. That is a promise on which you can stand.

....

....

....

....

....

....

....

....

When Judas, who had betrayed him, realized that Jesus had been condemned to die, he was filled with remorse. So he took the thirty pieces of silver back to the leading priests and the elders.
MATTHEW 27:3 NLT

Behind the Scenes

I know it is hard not to doubt Me. One of My closest followers did not believe it was Me when I rose from the grave. He had to touch My nail-scarred hands to be convinced it was really Me. It is much harder to believe when you cannot see or touch Me.

I am always with you. I am concerned about your day-to-day life. I love you, child. When you begin to doubt if I care, remember that I died for your sins. I took your place. I love you immensely.

Even when it seems like I am not moving, I am acting behind the scenes in your life. Trust Me to be who I say I am. I am Jesus, your Savior and your very best Friend. That will never change.

....

....

....

....

....

....

....

....

....

....

....

*Then he said to Thomas, "Put your finger here,
and look at my hands. Put your hand into the wound
in my side. Don't be faithless any longer. Believe!"*
JOHN 20:27 NLT

At Just the Right Time

I will always provide for you. Just as God provided a ram to be sacrificed in Isaac's place, I will provide for your needs at just the right time. It may seem like your story is playing out one way, but I can change its direction in an instant. I am not limited by what you can see. I am able to do immeasurably more than you can imagine.

Abraham was obedient. He took his beloved son and went up the mountain early in the morning. He did not want to kill his son, but he was prepared to sacrifice him, because this was God's command.

Be obedient. Strive to do My will and to use your gifts for My glory. Let Me handle the rest. Even when it seems like the outcome will be bleak, trust Me. I will provide.

....

....

....

....

....

....

....

....

....

....

Then Abraham lifted his eyes and looked, and there behind him was a ram caught in a thicket by its horns. So Abraham went and took the ram, and offered it up for a burnt offering instead of his son.
Genesis 22:13 nkjv

Always Available

I am always available. I am not like your family and friends, who are sometimes too busy to listen to you or to spend time with you. I do not sleep. My eyes are always roaming across the earth, looking for My faithful servants. I never tire of our conversations. I am interested in what interests you, and I want to know what you long for, what hurts, and what you need.

Call to Me throughout your day. Morning, noon, night, and anytime in between. Take a few moments to praise Me, to ask Me to be with you, or just to acknowledge Me. I walk with you through your day. I am in your workplace and in the car with you. I am always near, and I always hear your prayers.

....

....

....

....

....

....

....

....

....

....

As for me, I will call upon God, and the LORD shall save me.
Evening and morning and at noon I will pray,
and cry aloud, and He shall hear my voice.
PSALM 55:16–17 NKJV

Stop

You were knit together in your mother's womb. You are fully known and fully loved by Me. When you begin to plan out your life, keep in mind that you are not your own maker. You are My lamb. You were in My thoughts long before you came to be, and I have a bright future for you.

I have gifted you with certain talents and abilities that you can use to reach others for My kingdom. You are uniquely and wonderfully made. Nothing that I do is a mistake.

When your mind will not stop spinning and that lump in your throat says that there is no hope, no future, no change coming your way, stop. Remember whose you are. You belong to the King of this universe. You are Mine, and I am your Lord. I have great purposes for your life.

....

....

....

....

....

....

....

....

....

Know that the LORD, He is God; it is He who has made us, and not we ourselves; we are His people and the sheep of His pasture.
PSALM 100:3 NKJV

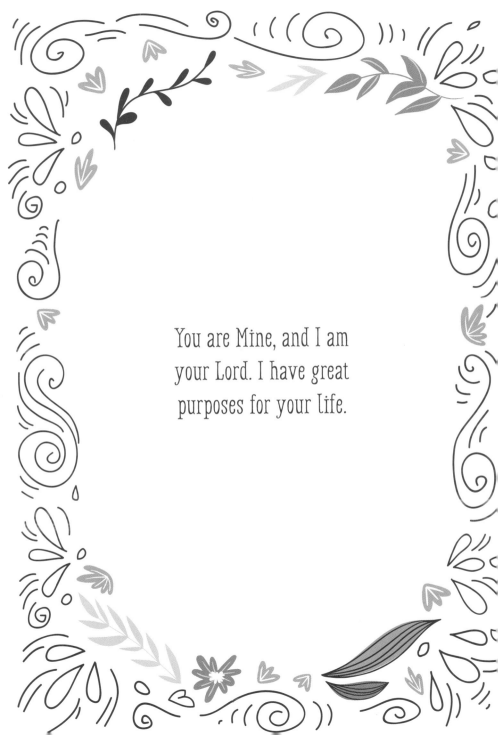

You are Mine, and I am your Lord. I have great purposes for your life.

Nothing Is Wasted

David knew what it meant to be afflicted. He was known as a man after God's own heart, but he made choices that took him down some bad roads. He was an adulterer and a murderer. Then he came back to God.

It is never fun to experience discipline or pain, but it does reap benefits down the road. You learn to spend time in My Word and in prayer. You may feel as if it is all you have. Sometimes I have to allow you to get to that point so that you will truly seek Me with your whole heart.

I do not take joy in seeing My children hurt. But I promise to use even this time of sorrow for your good. Nothing is wasted with Me. I work all things together for good in the lives of those who love Me.

It is good for me that I have been afflicted,
that I may learn Your statutes.
PSALM 119:71 NKJV

A Team

I will always lift you up. I place My hand beneath your chin and gently lift your head when you are down. Look up, My child! Always look up. This is where your help comes from. You are a child of heaven. You are Mine. You never have to feel ashamed or alone or abandoned. You are none of these. You are more than a conqueror, because I fight for you.

When it seems like everyone has left you, I haven't. When you feel alone and lonely, I stand ready to take your hand. When you cannot go one more step, allow your Savior to carry you. I am your Helper. I do not expect or desire for you to be strong. I will be your strength. Chin up! I am with you always, and we will do this together as a team.

I lift up my eyes to the mountains—where does my help come from?
My help comes from the LORD, the Maker of heaven and earth.
PSALM 121:1–2 NIV

I am powerful, and I
am your God. Trust Me
in your disappointment.

Something Great

In your disappointment, remember that My ways are not your ways. I have great plans for you, and sometimes I have to take things from your life in order to free up room for My blessings. You cling to something good—and sometimes even something really mediocre—when I want to give you something great.

I am the One who healed the sick and raised the dead back to life. I am still at work today, just as I was when I walked the earth, cleansing the leper of his sores and casting demons out of the possessed. I am powerful, and I am your God. Trust Me in your disappointment. I am working out My plan for you.

....

....

....

....

....

....

....

....

....

....

*"For my thoughts are not your thoughts, neither are
your ways my ways," declares the LORD. "As the heavens
are higher than the earth, so are my ways higher than
your ways and my thoughts than your thoughts."*
ISAIAH 55:8–9 NIV

You never need to doubt
that I hear your heart
when you pray.

You and Me

Have you ever noticed My teachings on prayer? Do I demand fancy words? Did I tell the people to memorize prayers from books and stand before the crowds reciting them? No. My desire is that you would find time to block out the world and tune in to Me, your great power source.

Prayer is just about you and Me. There is no agenda. There are no right words or correct sequences to follow. Just speak your heart to Me. Praise Me. Thank Me. Present your needs and requests to Me. Question Me, child. Cry to Me. And then. . .listen to Me. Prayer is a conversation.

You never need to worry about appearing simple or not having the right words. You never need to doubt that I hear your heart when you pray. I am not concerned with your vocabulary, but with your heart. I love you, child.

"But when you pray, go into your room, close the door and pray to your Father, who is unseen. Then your Father, who sees what is done in secret, will reward you."
MATTHEW 6:6 NIV

Angels Surround

Do you know how many times I have sent My angels to surround you? I protect you from dangers you never even see. I provide a way out for you when you are tempted. I constantly save you from the snares the evil one has set. He would love nothing more than to capture you with his lies and lure you away, but he has no power over you. Nothing can snatch you from My hand.

I hear you cry out to Me and ask Me why I would allow such disappointment to consume you. Know that your best interest is always on My mind. I am not out to get you or to harm you. I want to bless you, My precious one. You do not know the greater pain I may be saving you from, even though you have temporary discomfort.

Praise be to the LORD, who has not let us be torn by their teeth. We have escaped like a bird from the fowler's snare; the snare has been broken, and we have escaped.
PSALM 124:6–7 NIV

A Gift

Today truly is a gift—find the good in it. If you are feeling down, make a list of blessings that I have given you. Are you eating a warm meal today? Did you have a good night's sleep last night? Is there a family member or a friend whom you are thankful to have in your life? All of these are blessings straight from My hand.

There is an old song that reminds people to count their blessings and name them one by one. I am not a withholder of any good gift. I pour out My blessings in your life. Instead of seeing only what you lack, focus on all that you have. It will lift your spirits. A grateful heart is so attractive to those around you. They will see Me through your thankfulness even in the midst of grim circumstances.

....

....

....

....

....

....

....

....

....

....

This is the day the LORD has made. We will rejoice and be glad in it.
PSALM 118:24 NLT

Know that one day you will
be fully healed and complete in
heaven. This is My will for you.

Fully Healed

Physical ailments can really bring you down. A chronic illness or pain can lead to depression. It is understandable, and yet there is always hope.

Even if your body doesn't work like it used to and you are left feeling like you will never be the same, take heart. One day you will have a brand-new, spiritual body. It will be perfect and glorious.

You are weak, child, but I am strong. Today, ask Me to give you the energy you need to face discomforts and disease. I may or may not heal your physical body on earth. Trust Me to do what is right for you, even if you don't understand. Know that one day you will be fully healed and complete in heaven. This is My will for you.

....
....
....
....
....
....
....
....
....
....
....

He will take our weak mortal bodies and change them
into glorious bodies like his own, using the same power
with which he will bring everything under his control.
PHILIPPIANS 3:21 NLT

Your Real Home

As long as you are living and breathing in a fallen world, there will be disappointment, hurt, and loss. It may seem that you have received a greater dose of sorrow than your friends or loved ones. Try not to compare yourself to others. Just as a parent deals with each of his children individually, I meet the needs of those God has entrusted to Me. It may not always seem fair, but it is always right.

You are experiencing homesickness, child. Your real home is heaven, and one day you will have a new body and be in your new home. Have faith. That day is coming. In the meantime, meet frustrations with boldness. Know that I work even through your hurts.

....

....

....

....

....

....

....

....

So we are always confident, even though we know that as long as we live in these bodies we are not at home with the Lord. For we live by believing and not by seeing. Yes, we are fully confident, and we would rather be away from these earthly bodies, for then we will be at home with the Lord.
2 CORINTHIANS 5:6–8 NLT

A Marvelous Place

I do not see death the same way you do. Death lost its sting the day I rose from the grave. Death died that day. There is no death for the Christian; there is only the passing from one life to the next. The new life that awaits you is so glorious that you will never wish to return to earth once you are with Me in heaven.

When believers die, it is the ones who are left behind who grieve. The believers are now in their eternal home. The angels rejoice at their homecoming. Loved ones who are already here in heaven greet their beloved ones. Life on earth seems but a blink of an eye to the newcomers when they pass through heaven's gates.

Child, heaven is what you wait for. It is what you long for, even if you don't know it. Trust Me. Do not be afraid of death. I have prepared a marvelous place for you.

....

....

....

....

....

....

....

....

....

....

Precious in the sight of the LORD is the death of his faithful servants.
PSALM 116:15 NIV

Those who do not trust in
Me will live out their days
in a dry land, but you, child,
are like a tree planted by a river.

My Own

I give families to those who are lonely. I set prisoners free. I defend those who cannot defend themselves. I am not limited by the boundaries of human strength or ability. I am Jesus. I am the Son of the Living God.

I have called you My own and I am faithful and trustworthy. You may not have been able to trust your earthly father. You can trust in Me. Maybe you lost your husband. You won't lose Me. I will be all that you need. I will be your Comforter and Healer. I will be your Prince of Peace when you are anxious and your Shield when Satan comes against you with his lies.

Those who do not trust in Me will live out their days in a dry land, but you, child, are like a tree planted by a river.

....

....

....

....

....

....

....

....

....

....

God is in his holy Temple. He is a father to orphans, and he defends the widows. God gives the lonely a home. He leads prisoners out with joy, but those who turn against God will live in a dry land.
PSALM 68:5–6 NCV

Turn to Me

You can be lonely even in a house full of people. You can feel completely satisfied when all alone. Loneliness is a state of mind, not so much about how many bodies are in the room. Everyone experiences loneliness at times. It is part of being human.

When you are lonely, turn to Me. Literally turn to Me, child. Go to your knees or curl up in that big armchair and meet with Me. I am just a prayer away. As you talk with Me, ask Me to fill the void in you. There is, you know, a God-shaped hole in all humans. It cannot be filled with anyone or anything but Me.

Loneliness serves a great purpose. It draws you closer to your Messiah. It allows Me to meet your needs and to minister to you. I love you.

Turn to me and be gracious to me, for I am lonely and afflicted.
PSALM 25:16 NIV

Grace-Bearer

Discretion. Good sense. Integrity. No matter what you call it, it serves a person well. When you can stop in the heat of the moment and take a deep breath, you are showing wisdom. Be slow to anger.

One of the greatest ways that you can be a witness for Me is through your love. It is a piece of cake to love those who love you. It is easy to be compassionate and giving toward those who treat you well.

What about the one who has wounded your heart? What about the one who deserves a good tongue-lashing? When you overlook an offense—however small or great—you are showing discretion. I see the way that another has hurt you. No wrongdoing goes unnoticed by your Savior. There is a thing called grace. You are a recipient of it. Be also a bearer of it time and time again. Seventy times seven. It will serve you well.

A man's discretion makes him slow to anger,
and it is his glory to overlook a transgression.
PROVERBS 19:11 NASB

The Golden Rule

"Treat others as you want to be treated" is a saying you probably have heard all of your life. Some call it the Golden Rule. It is a simple statement, but hard to live by.

When you fail, do you want to be forgiven? When you have hurt someone, do you wish you could take the words or actions back? All have sinned. All fall short of the glory of God. You are not alone.

So when people wound you with their words, remember that your words have wounded someone along the way too. When you are rejected, consider that someone may have felt rejected by you in the past. Have you been shown grace? If not, would forgiveness have been like a glass of cold water on a hot summer day?

I have poured out mercy upon you. While you were yet a sinner, I died for you. From those to whom much has been given, much is required. Treat others with the unmerited favor you have received.

"Do to others as you would like them to do to you."
Luke 6:31 nlt

Mine Forever

I know all about being rejected. I was rejected by many people. They did not believe that I was the Son of God. In the end, even My own disciples disowned Me. They said they didn't know Me. They hid in the shadows as I died on the cross. They didn't understand.

Do not let rejection define you. Your friends or even your own family members may abandon you. They may struggle with inner demons or addictions that limit their ability to love. They may want to be close to you, but their own spirits may keep them at a distance due to wounds they bear.

I know there is a sting that comes with abandonment. It is so hard to be left by someone you trusted. Know that even if your parents, children, or spouse reject you, I will never abandon you. You are Mine forever and ever, and it is My delight to be your Lord and your Friend.

For my father and my mother have forsaken me,
but the LORD will take me up.
PSALM 27:10 NASB

Focus on walking closely
with Me and worshipping Me.
I will bless you with the
desires of your heart.

The Desires of Your Heart

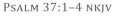

You may wonder why it seems that those who come against you prosper while you continue to wait for a blessing. Trust My timing and My heart. I have not forgotten you.

Just because I don't instantly punish someone doesn't mean I have not seen his wrongdoing. My ways, remember, are higher than your own. I am gracious. I give second chances, and third, and fourth. . . . If someone continues in a lifestyle that is blatantly evil, do not worry. Such a person will experience My wrath in due time. Don't envy others.

Trust Me to do what is right for you. Focus on walking closely with Me and worshipping Me. I will bless you with the desires of your heart.

....

....

....

....

....

....

....

....

....

Do not fret because of evildoers, nor be envious of the workers of iniquity. For they shall soon be cut down like the grass, and wither as the green herb. Trust in the LORD, and do good; dwell in the land, and feed on His faithfulness. Delight yourself also in the LORD, and He shall give you the desires of your heart.
PSALM 37:1–4 NKJV

The Cost

Has someone persecuted you for being a believer? Maybe it has not been nearly as drastic as what Stephen experienced, but you may have suffered for My name. Be assured that any suffering you endure for My name's sake will be rewarded in heaven.

Stephen was put to death for speaking the truth. He was stoned, killed in a horrendous way, and yet he prayed for those who murdered him. He saw Me standing at the right hand of the Father, and he knew where he was going. He was worried for the souls of those who threw rocks at him. That is a compassionate heart.

Consider the cost of following Me. If it is worth it to you, then count it an honor to stand for My name even unto death.

....

....

....

....

....

....

....

....

....

They went on stoning Stephen as he called on the Lord and said, "Lord Jesus, receive my spirit!" Then falling on his knees, he cried out with a loud voice, "Lord, do not hold this sin against them!" Having said this, he fell asleep.
ACTS 7:59–60 NASB

Compassion

When one member of a family hurts, everyone hurts. It should be the same with the body of Christ. Practice carrying others' burdens as if they were your own. You should be so filled with compassion when a Christian brother or sister is hurting that you are moved to action.

I was called to lay down My life for mankind. Likewise, you should lay down your own desires and look to the needs of others. See to the orphans and widows. Look for those in your fellowship who are lonely or facing challenges. Visit them. Seek out those who are depressed. A kind word or a smile can go a long way. See others' burdens as your own. This pleases Me, child.

Carry each other's burdens, and in this
way you will fulfill the law of Christ.
GALATIANS 6:2 NIV

Givers

People who give are often not appreciated. You may have given until you had nothing left to give and yet found yourself rejected by those you served. You may be totally spent from doing for others and yet have never received one single "thank you." I understand.

I healed ten men of the terrible disease of leprosy. One offered a word of thanks.

I was not the king the people were looking for. They wanted fanfare and pageantry, but I rode into town on a donkey. They knew not what they beheld when they looked into My eyes. If they had looked a bit deeper, they would have seen the love and grace that stared back at them.

I experienced rejection. I was unappreciated. I understand that kind of pain. Hold on, My child. A day is coming when you will receive your reward. Do not give up on doing good.

_He was despised and rejected by mankind, a man of suffering,
and familiar with pain. Like one from whom people hide their
faces he was despised, and we held him in low esteem._
ISAIAH 53:3 NIV

Hold on, My child. A day
is coming when you will
receive your reward.

No Record of Wrongs

You know that person who injured your spirit, child? The one who said those hateful things and let you down? You know that individual against whom you have held a grudge for too long? Consider letting the bitterness go today. Forgiveness is a choice. It may not come easy. You may pick up that resentment again tomorrow and have to try forgiveness again. But it is always a choice.

Just as the father ran to meet his prodigal son, reach out in forgiveness to the person who hurt you. Harboring hatred does nothing for you or for the other person. If your pride keeps you from forgiving, it is time to lay down your pride, child. Love keeps no record of wrongs, even really bad ones. Even the wrongs that sting your very soul. When you let them go, you will find healing.

"But while he was still a long way off, his father saw him and was filled with compassion for him; he ran to his son, threw his arms around him and kissed him."
LUKE 15:20 NIV

See Me

In your own strength, you cannot please Me. But when you rely on the working of the Holy Spirit within you, it is possible. Walk in My ways. Follow My statutes. Seek My face in all matters. I will cover you with My protection. When others see you, they will see Me. Even your enemies will recognize My favor upon your life. They will want to be at peace with you.

My children stand out in a crowd. It is not the way that they walk through the good times that is unique. It is their reaction to adversity that really attracts the nonbelievers around them. Live in the power of the Holy Spirit. Follow hard after Me all of your days. Walk humbly and do good to all people. I will take care of the rest. I will bless you and keep you.

....

....

....

....

....

....

....

....

....

When a man's ways please the LORD, He makes
even his enemies to be at peace with him.
PROVERBS 16:7 NKJV

Pick You Up

A good father will stoop to carry his child when the child grows too tired to walk. Imagine the father carrying the child high upon his shoulders. This is how I carry you. I know that you are weak and that the world throws a lot of curveballs your way. I know that there are hurts and disappointments that cause you to stumble. I am here to pick you up, dust you off, and put you on the right path again.

I do not expect you to be perfect. I just want you to walk with Me and stay close to My side. I know that you are human. I made you. I know everything about you. I will be your strength when you are weak. Let Me be your strength.

....

....

....

....

....

....

....

....

....

....

As a father pities his children, so the Lord pities those who fear Him.
For He knows our frame; He remembers that we are dust.
Psalm 103:13–14 nkjv

I See Your Heart

Being falsely accused or misunderstood is always hurtful. Joseph was set up by Potiphar's wife. He was framed. Potiphar threw him into prison, but God was with him there. God showed him favor even in prison.

You may feel as though you have been misunderstood or even blatantly falsely accused of doing something you did not do. Know that even when others treat you unfairly, I am with you. I am able to bless you and bring good from any situation. There is no set of circumstances that is too dismal for Me to work through, child.

Often it is best to simply be still. Rather than defending yourself, let your character speak for itself. I see your heart. You can find favor with Me regardless of what others think or say.

....

....

....

....

....

....

....

....

....

Then Joseph's master took him and put him into the prison,
a place where the king's prisoners were confined. And he was there
in the prison. But the LORD was with Joseph and showed him mercy,
and He gave him favor in the sight of the keeper of the prison.
GENESIS 39:20–21 NKJV

Opportunities

You have a limited number of days on the earth, child. Every day ordained for you is written in My book. There will come a day when you leave life as you know it to enter your eternal home in heaven.

Since life is short and each day is a gift, try to find the good in each twenty-four hours you receive. Pray that you will be a blessing to someone who is hurting each day. Look for opportunities to show My love.

On your dark days, it is easy to wish life away. You wonder if you can make it through another week to the weekend. You count the days until your next vacation.

Life is a gift from Me, child—learn to see it that way. I want you to make each day count. I want you to have an abundant life.

Teach us to realize the brevity of life, so that we may grow in wisdom.
Psalm 90:12 NLT

Selflessness

You are building a reputation for yourself. Every day, you stack another brick onto the structure with your words and actions. When you get too absorbed with your own troubles and longings, a brick called self-absorption is added. When you look outside yourself to see and to meet the needs of others, a brick called selflessness is added.

When people look at your life, do they see a godly person who finds the good in every situation and is always seeking to please Me? Or do they see a downcast soul, one who thinks only of her own problems?

You want to leave a godly legacy. You want to be known as one who followed hard after your Savior. I know this is the desire of your heart. Make sure that your actions match that desire.

We have happy memories of the godly,
but the name of a wicked person rots away.
Proverbs 10:7 nlt

Live in the power of the
Holy Spirit. Follow hard
after Me all of your days.

Great Deliverer

I am not only your Savior from sin—I am also your great Deliverer. I watch over your life and keep you from danger. When you are at your wits' end, when the day could not be any darker, when you feel you literally cannot go on, I am there. I will deliver you not just once, but again and again.

Set your hope not on things of the world. Money and material possessions will only bring temporary happiness. When you are facing the trials of life, the hardships, or your final moments, you will not call upon those things. You will call upon Me.

Do not set your hope on other people. They are great blessings to your life, but they are not your salvation or your sustenance. I am.

Trust Me, child. I will deliver you.

....

....

....

....

....

....

....

....

....

....

He has delivered us from such a deadly peril, and he will deliver us again. On him we have set our hope that he will continue to deliver us.
2 Corinthians 1:10 niv

Ask Me

Jabez was said to be more honorable than his brothers. He was given his name by his mother, who had a painful childbirth experience when he was born. Jabez means "sorrowful" or "sorrow-maker." He prayed to be protected from pain and sorrow. He asked for a blessing, and his prayer was heard and answered.

The prayer of Jabez also includes a request that God's hand would be with him. He knew that he needed protection and guidance. Jabez knew where every good gift came from, and he knew his source of strength.

I will be with you, child. Ask Me. Come before Me and earnestly seek My will. I delight in answering your prayers.

....
....
....
....
....
....
....
....
....

Jabez cried out to the God of Israel, "Oh, that you would bless me and enlarge my territory! Let your hand be with me, and keep me from harm so that I will be free from pain." And God granted his request.
1 Chronicles 4:10 niv

Come before Me and earnestly seek My will. I delight in answering your prayers.

Right and Pleasing

I know it seems like the bad guy always gets what the good guy deserves. I know you sometimes feel like you're losing the battle. I get it. Suffering is never easy. It is so hard to suffer for doing the right thing, while people who have done wrong seem to benefit.

In the end, all things will be made right. Trust Me. Continue to do what is right and pleasing to Me. It will be worth it in the end. You will reap far greater benefits by doing things the right way rather than looking for shortcuts.

I am so proud of you when you stand up for Me and take the heat for it. It is not always the popular thing to do, but it is always right. I am pleased when I see you making good choices regardless of the immediate outcome.

If you suffer for doing good and you endure it,
this is commendable before God.
1 PETER 2:20 NIV

The Narrow Path

Keep going. It may seem like those who disregard My name are prospering, but in the end you will see this isn't true. I want you to continue to be faithful, child. Continue doing good in My name. Don't give up on My ways. Follow the guidelines I have given you in My Word. The scriptures will never lead you astray.

There are people who take shortcuts and see gray on topics where My Word is black and white. These are not My ways. These are not the ways of the Christian.

Stay on the narrow path. There are fewer walking on this path, but it is the way that leads to true reward. I love you, child, and I want the very best for you. Your faithfulness to Me does not go unseen. It will not go unrewarded.

....

....

....

....

....

....

....

....

....

The faithless will be fully repaid for their ways,
and the good rewarded for theirs.
PROVERBS 14:14 NIV

Wait. . .

Waiting is not easy. It can be a very frustrating process, particularly if it takes a long time. I know that you are waiting for Me to do a great thing in your life. Be patient, even when it seems that you have been waiting forever.

I promised Sarah a child, and she bore one in her old age. Noah built an ark, and the floods came, just as I said. I keep My Word, child. I have your future in My hands, just as I have promised. I am the Giver of all good gifts. I know the plans I have for you, plans to give you hope and a bright future.

Wait for Me. In the meantime, allow Me to be your Helper. I am always near.

....
....
....
....
....
....
....
....
....
....
....

We wait in hope for the Lord; he is our help and our shield.
PSALM 33:20 NIV

Guard Your Heart

I tell you to guard your heart, child. This does not mean you have to construct walls and never let anyone in. It simply means that you must be cautious. Be sure that you know people before you let them into your heart. When your heart is broken, it takes time to heal. You are not able to serve Me at your very best in such a state.

Put your heart into the things that really matter in this life. Do not waste your affections on material things like money. Invest your energy, attention, and even your emotions wisely. There is only so much time in a day and only so many things you can say yes to. Use discernment in making these choices.

Guard your heart. It is the part of you from which life flows.

....
....
....
....
....
....
....
....
....
....
....
....

Above all else, guard your heart, for everything you do flows from it.
PROVERBS 4:23 NIV

Look for Me today. I am always near. Peace be with you, My child.

Look for Me

I appeared to many people after My resurrection. They were shocked. Some thought they were seeing a ghost. They did not understand when I told them that I would rise after three days, so they were stunned when the prophecy came true.

Some believed Me automatically. Others, like Thomas, took some time to be convinced that it was really Me.

Do you recognize Me when I come to you, child? I may not appear to you in bodily form as I did to My disciples and others after My resurrection, but I do appear to you.

I come to you through a friend who calls at just the right time when you are feeling low. I come to you in creation when I paint glorious sunsets in the sky that remind you of My greatness.

Look for Me today. I am always near. Peace be with you, My child.

....

....

....

....

....

....

....

....

While they were still talking about this, Jesus himself stood among them and said to them, "Peace be with you." They were startled and frightened, thinking they saw a ghost.
LUKE 24:36–37 NIV

Right Where You Are

Try not to look back and wonder whether you have made the right decisions. It is easy to go down the trail of asking, *Did I marry the right person?* or, *Would I have been happier if I had stayed in my previous job?*

I have you right where you are for a reason. I am more than capable of using everything in your life, even the wrong turns or mistakes, for good.

Looking back with rose-colored glasses makes the past look more appealing than the present. But if you dwell on the past, you will miss out on what I am doing. I am doing a new thing in your life. I never stop working. I never cease to bring new people and opportunities into your life. Trust Me. Let's go forward together.

....
....
....
....
....
....
....
....
....
....

Do not say, "Why were the old days better than these?"
For it is not wise to ask such questions.
ECCLESIASTES 7:10 NIV

Speak My Name

When you are hurting, be still. Come before Me and simply speak My name. Rest in My presence. I demand nothing of you but your time. Seek Me and you will find Me. Draw near to Me and I will hold you close.

The deeper the hurt, the more time you need to spend in My presence. I do not delight in your tears. They hurt My heart. But your pain causes you to lean more fully upon Me. This is right where I want you, fully dependent on your Savior.

I want to be Lord of your life. I ask that you surrender every area to Me, not holding back just one or two that you think you can handle better. Lay down your burdens and be still. I am your Lord. I will take care of you. This is My job.

....

....

....

....

....

....

....

....

....

....

....

He says, "Be still, and know that I am God; I will be exalted among the nations, I will be exalted in the earth."
PSALM 46:10 NIV

Routines

Establish routines in your life, child. Create routines that include prayer and time in My word. These will serve you well when you encounter days of catastrophe or heartache.

Daniel was in the habit of praying regularly. He was disciplined in this. So when the king ordered that no one should pray to other gods, Daniel knew what to do. He disregarded this and went right on with his routine. He came straight to Me. He wasn't about to be detoured by an earthly king and lose sight of his heavenly Lord.

Learn from Daniel. Choose a time of day—or more than one—that you will come before Me in prayer. Stick to it. No matter what hurts or disappointments come your way, establish this routine and keep it. It will make such a difference in your life.

....

....

....

....

....

....

....

*Now when Daniel learned that the decree had been published,
he went home to his upstairs room where the windows opened toward
Jerusalem. Three times a day he got down on his knees and prayed,
giving thanks to his God, just as he had done before.*
DANIEL 6:10 NIV

Journal Your Way to a Deeper Faith

The 5-Minute Prayer Plan Journal for Women

Many Christians yearn for a dynamic prayer life, but we often get stuck in a repetitive routine of prayer. This practical and inspirational journal will give you new ways to approach prayer with 90 focused 5-minute plans for your daily quiet time. These prayer plans explore a variety of life themes appropriate for women of all ages.

Spiral Bound / 978-1-64352-506-8 / $9.99

More Jesus: A Devotional Journal

More than 100 devotional readings and prayers fill this journal—touching on topics like illness, anxiety, loss, failure, and worry—will breathe fresh hope and peace into your spirit on the difficult days *and* every day in between.

Flexible Casebound / 978-1-64352-899-1 / $12.99